The Route

Copyright © 2001 Kevin C. Wilson
All rights reserved.

ISBN 0-9716830-0-X

The Route

Kevin C. Wilson

Barnyard Books
Title No. 001
2001

The Route

To my Nutcracker

Kevin C. [signature]

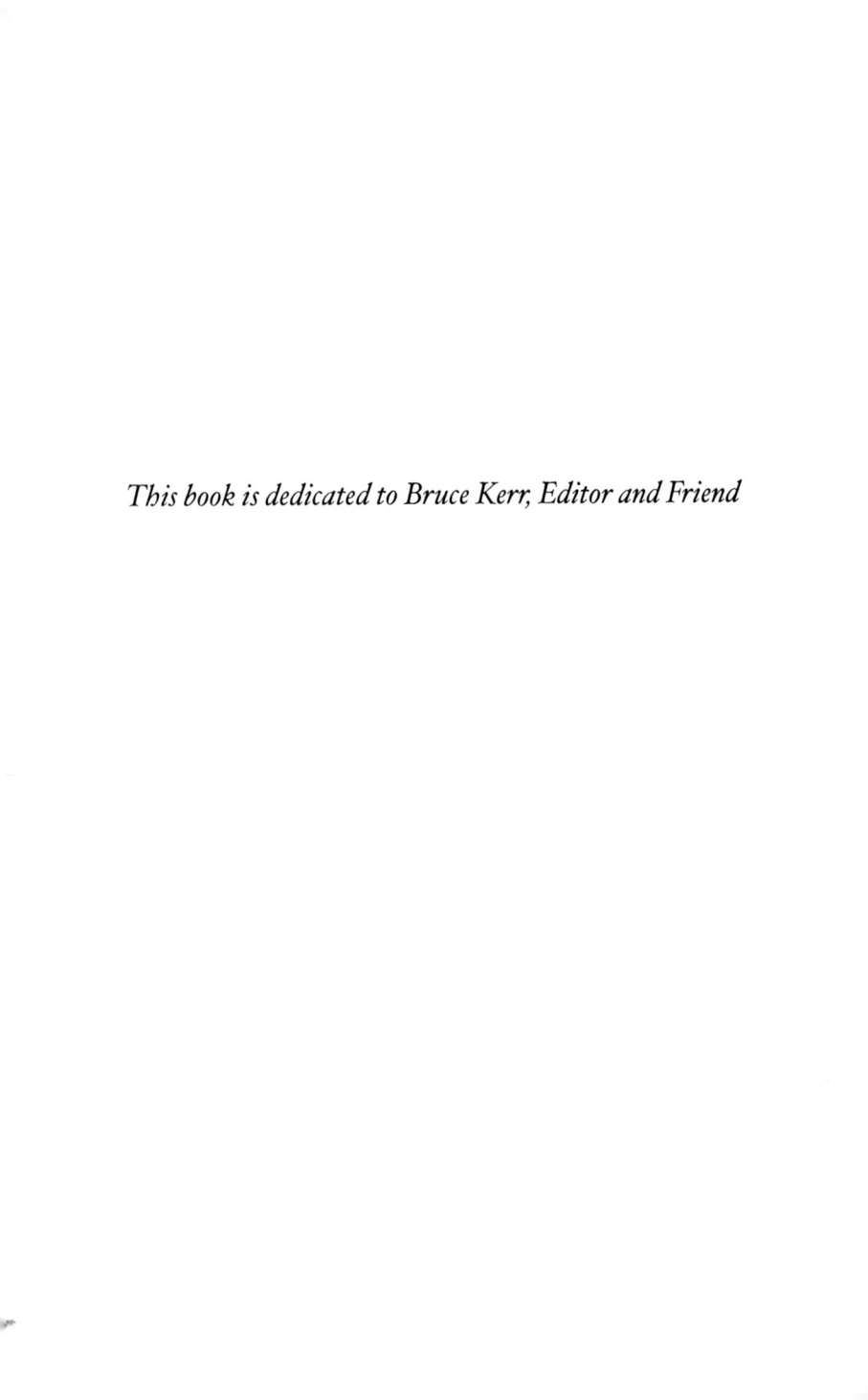

This book is dedicated to Bruce Kerr, Editor and Friend

"Has any ill befallen old Pittheus? He is well on in life yet I should be sorry if he left us."

-Euripides

Lines from "A Tiny Little Town" by Bruce Kerr: 1991 by Bruce Kerr. Used by permission.

Lines from "Me O Me O" by Walter Fixsen: 1991 by Walter Fixsen. Used by permission.

Lines from "Fourteen Days" by Steven E. Guest: 1991 by Steven E. Guest. Used by permission.

Contents

I

1: Four Hundred Pounds of Love and Squalor, or "It Wasn't Always Like This"
2: "Is That You, Gerald?" or "What'd I Tell You?"
3: Mandingo and Maud, or "Can This Be Love?"
4: Bingo and Booze, or "It's Not a Pretty Picture."
5: The Deadbeat Hotel, or Home Sweet Home
6: The Secret of the Pink House, or Piano Lust, Part One
7: A Day Late, or A Dollar Short
8: My Three Sons, or Blues For a Family
9: The Make Do Band, or Neighborhood Tunes
10: The White Picket Fence, or The Black Cat
11: The Worst Band in the World, or Meet the Rubes

II

12: Dinner with the Goodnights, or Can't Buy Me Love
13: An Elongated Concept of Time, or A Couple More Days
14: Home Away From Home, or Return of the Stumbler
15: Bit Part Player, or The Ghoul
16: The Peter Foster Film Festival, or The Actor That Wouldn't Die
17: The Queen of the Georgia Package, or "Et tu, Lar?"
18: Detox, or Delay
19: Voris' Chest, or "Which Mrs. Ferguson?"
20: Ticket To Ride, or "Thanks for the Memories"

III

21: The Rubes-Live, or Let There Be Drums
22: Decline and Fall of the Deadbeat Hotel, or Calling All Rubes
23: Vagrant or Vagabond
24: or Knock on Any Door

Chapter One
Four Hundred Pounds of Love and Squalor, or "It Wasn't Always Like This"

"Did I pay you?"

The loaded question floated in the air above the kitchen table, behind which Frances' girth was more or less distributed across the expanse of three kitchen chairs drawn close together. The wooden spindles creaked when she shifted, but apparently the glue was still holding where I'd fixed those chairs.

She hadn't paid me for the chairs, a nearly forgotten project, nor for painting the ceiling on the screened porch, nor for the twenty-three bags of leaves I'd raked out of her back yard and carried to the curb in front.

My chances of collecting on any of these were close to fifty-fifty.

She was in one of her rare moods. The neck of the liter I'd brought back for her from the liquor store was peeping out of the brown paper bag on the table, yet to be opened. She had a mid-morning glow on, her silvery voice guilelessly sincere, dulcet tones tinkling all over the place. She could be charming, Frances, on occasion. This wasn't one of them.

She knew I'd kept the change from the twenty after pedaling her tricycle to the liquor store and back. A mile each way. Six bucks. Big deal. Three eighty-five of that bought a pint of Dark Eyes for my trouble. A couple of bucks for cigarettes. What was left? About twenty cents. She was referring to that and if I said yes, she'd figure we were square on everything and I'd never get paid for the ceiling, the lawn work, or the chairs.

Not that that was the least of my worries. Sure, I could use a few bucks, times being what they were, but whether Frances paid me now or later or not at all, the simple fact that she owed me would remain. Her guilt was like having a very small amount of money in the bank.

Next thing I knew I had agreed to paint her fence. God only knew how long it would take to scrape a hundred and sixty-seven pickets. No room in the budget for a primer coat. For fifty bucks, one coat had to cover. If she wanted to pay for a restoration project, I could spend the rest of the summer scraping peeling paint. The fence, last painted circa 1951, deserved my full attention, but for twenty-nine cents a picket, it was not going to get it.

In a mental file I made a note to be around on the second of the month when Delbert's check was due. Frances wrote most of her checks for the month within the first five days of the month. She'd get a spurt of generosity and bestow an absurd amount on some cabdriver, then she'd tighten up and get crafty for the next three weeks. Most of the time, that was where I came in. But it wasn't always like this.

That phrase cropped up a lot on my route. I even said it myself, like someone succumbing to a fit of retrospection, as if the bygone days were in reality so much better.

In my case, of course, they were. How the mighty have fallen, and so on. I couldn't afford to dwell on former glories for long, so I listened at some distance with empathy toward Frances when she waxed nostalgic toward the past. And though it was a nightmare world inside her domicile, with Delbert in the living room watching The Flintstones in his underpants, a can of beer in his hand and the husky fetor of bowel sickness thickening the air around his bearlike mindless body, I scarcely raised an eyebrow anymore at the squalor.

"You may not believe this," Frances was saying, "in fact, I don't know why I'm even telling you, unless it's because there's just no one else to tell, but there was a time when Mr. Delbert and me would take off all our clothes and dance naked right here in this kitchen. No, it wasn't always like this."

She nodded toward the lumpish vegetable in the recliner, mesmerized by the cartoons, her eyes going suddenly moist until she picked up the nearest throwable item, an empty ketchup bottle, and bounced it with a careless grace off his chair, causing him to jump up with a start and look around, muttering, "What? What?"

"Shut up," Frances bellowed at him. She grinned at me. "That gets him."

Delbert grunted, "You shut up." Frances poured me a drink of her bourbon, put a little cola in it and some ice. With a sly squint she studied me.

"I paid you, right?" she said.

"Not yet," I said.

Her tone sharpened. "I paid you, mister."

"Not for everything. The back porch ceiling? That was what, twenty bucks?"

"Now I heard it. How many times you going to charge me for that ceiling?"

"What about the yardwork, Frances? Twenty-three bags of leaves. Come on. Not one nickel for that. And never mind the chairs I fixed. Just throw them in. The wood glue cost me a dollar nineteen with tax, but it was worth it to be able to do you a favor, Frances." I fixed her with what was meant to be an impenetrable stare.

Undeterred, she said, "you think I don't remember? You think I don't remember writing you a check for all that?"

"Do you remember stopping payment on it?"

"Did I do that?" Shock and amazement.

"Every so often you do, Frances, yes. You did it to me last time. I haven't forgotten."

"Well, maybe I did," she said.

"You shouldn't do that, Frances," I said.

"Shame on me," she tittered.

I was prepared to badger a check out of her one way or another, but she reached for her checkbook without further ado, so I curtailed the poor working man shtick.

"How much for the lawnwork? What did you say, twenty-three bags? Let's see, that's about six bags an hour, right? About ten minutes a bag? That's four hours work at your regular rate, what's minimum wage?" She licked a pencil and started figuring.

"Three-eighty-five an hour, but Frances, eight hours in the hot sun."

"I know how you work," she said, as she scribbled her figures on a paper plate stained with traces of nacho cheese. "That's $15.40. We'll call it fifteen, even, and twenty for the back porch ceiling, and the chairs are free, right?"

"A dollar nineteen for the glue."

"Thirty-six dollars and nineteen cents," she said. "Geez, you make me tired with your moneygrubbing extras. Here, I thought you were a friend of mine."

Clearly, it pained her to write the check. She held it out to me as if to take it from her were a betrayal. My fingers closed on it as I stood to make my exit.

"Take the money and run," she said. "Like you do. Don't worry about me, I'll be fine."

A careful examination confirmed that the check contained no errors. "Frances," I said, "please don't cancel this one."

"Maybe I will and maybe I won't," she said. "You won't know till you go to the bank, will you?" That struck her as hilarious.

"You want that fence painted, don't you?"

She let out a great guffaw. "That'll be the day I give a damn about that fence."

She was still laughing as I let myself out. The air in the street outside was like pure oxygen. The folded check in my pocket was like a compass needle pointing my steps in a walking beeline to the bank. "It wasn't always like this," I kept thinking. "It wasn't always like this."

Chapter Two
"Is That You, Gerald?" or "What Did I Tell You?"

As I stood in the bank endorsing the check, it struck me that the date, the twentieth of May, was Clarence's birthday. He'd have been ninety-three.

On his last day, I was in the next room at his house, sitting in my customary chair at the table on his porch, typing a letter to a friend. If he'd been in any pain, or called out, I would have heard his reedy voice. My ear was tuned to his least whisper.

For a year I had lived there with him. He needed a keeper, someone to look out for him, run his errands for him and keep him from driving his car. At the age of ninety-two, he had absolutely no trouble renewing his driver's license. An eye test was deemed unnecessary, despite the obvious difficulty he had distinguishing colors and shapes of signs. One ride with him was sufficient for me to recognize it as my duty to protect the community from the menace he became in traffic.

Luckily the stores were within walking distance. Years had passed since I drove a car. Not that I couldn't, I just never renewed my license. For one thing, I had little need of a car, having come to rely on public transportation and walking a great deal. After Jenny left me little details like renewing licenses and insurance policies came to represent only fees I could ill afford to pay.

I wish I could say here that I embarked on a quest or a voyage at that point, or even that I devoted my talents, such as they were, to a higher purpose. I may have intended, once, to try to excuse, in so many words, a damnable string of setbacks, but I make no more excuses to my sons. They know where I failed them and where I stood them right. I tried to be a good dad. I let them down in so many ways, but I tried, at least, to make up for my failures in other ways. They know I'm still trying.

They know I'd sleep on the beach before imposing on them. That's why I ended up at Clarence's when the boys got their own apartment together. They didn't need old dad in the way.

Clarence did need somebody. He was close to needing a full-time private nurse, which would have cost him plenty. In the end, he started calling me Gerald.

Gerald was his son in Germany. He called once and was rude when I answered. "What," he asked, "was the nature of my business with his father?" My answer, that I was Mr. Clarence's butler, did not please him. Clarence held the phone away from his ear and I could hear Gerald yelling from across the ocean at his father, who was deaf as a post when he wanted to be. Clarence was still sharp in those days. He kept saying, "What?" into the phone, until Gerald hung up on him.

Clarence often conveyed a little half-smile when he had amused himself by aggravating somebody. He might have been considering whether to try to pretend to me that he didn't know who he'd been talking to, or listening to, as he replaced the receiver with a fumbling dexterity. When he looked at me, I was looking at him.

"How about a drink, Pete?" he said.

He couldn't reach into the icebox anymore without great effort, so I fixed the drinks. He liked bourbon, a very light splash, with water and I drank vodka with coke. We sat on the porch looking out across the street. Voris Fletcher was out in her yard, watering her plants. She had on a sunbonnet with a red bow on the straw. She waved at the two of us and smiled. All very neighborly.

"Pete," said Clarence, in one of his rare expansive moments, "you know Voris is a widow woman."

That much I knew about her, yes.

"She's got no family living. No children."

He had my undivided attention.

"Her husband, Dr. Ray Fletcher, left her pretty well fixed. She owns that house and I happen to know she's got a fair little portfolio of blue chip stock. I knew Ray Fletcher well. He was a fine man. Known them both for thirty years. He took good care of her. And Voris worked her whole life, too. Twenty years at Sunset Bank. She retired a few years ago, right before Ray died." Clarence took his time between sentences. I'd learned not to rush him. "She went a little dotty after that, but she's all right, to look at her. How old would you say she is?

She looked about my age, a little older. "Late fifties, early sixties?"

"She's almost seventy." Clarence looked at me with something close to pity, as if he hoped he didn't have to spell it out any further for me.

We had discussed venture capital before. He knew about my screenplay and my plan to raise venture capital for an independent production. He wasn't interested himself, but he saw it quicker than I did, how the whole situation was there, ripe for the picking, that idle afternoon as we sat talking and drinking and watching Voris moving through the shade of her botanical garden. I'd mown her lawn for her several times and she was always kind and congenial toward me. Certain of future work around her house in the nature of gardening, yardwork, or painting, I slept secure in the notion that she would continue to allow me to be her yardman of choice.

Feelings of surprise and disappointment were my initial reactions when a couple of young black fellows on bicycles rode up dragging a lawnmower and proceeded to mow her lawn.

"Looks like you've got competition, Pete," said Clarence. "You better get in there before they do. There's your venture capital, right across the street."

At the time I was appalled at Clarence's insinuation that I would even contemplate such a course of action. No, I told him, it was not my style to separate elderly widows from their retirement security. I was pursuing other avenues, to wit, the letter I was in the midst of writing to a friend of mine in Las Vegas, Rico Caminiti, who was with me all the way on the movie deal.

The financing was in the works but it took time. Meanwhile, I needed just enough to hang in there, body and soul money.

My code of conduct prevented me from seizing a number of dubious opportunities, such as the one Clarence was pointing out to me with calculating delight.

"Not my style," I repeated.

Neither of us could have known the portent of that conversation. Not even Clarence could have guessed how Voris would change in the months to come.

Every morning I walked to the store to get cigarettes. As I passed her house I would pick up her morning paper where the paperboy had left it at the foot of her driveway and give it a practiced fling over her chain link fence and watch it drop like an apple on her front porch. Just something I liked to do for her, to save her a few steps. She asked me once if I would be her security guard. With no idea what she had in mind, I said, "Certainly, Voris, if you will explain to me what my duties would entail." She wasn't quite sure, herself. But she was concerned about the security of her home. She didn't feel safe in it.

Though I knew nothing about security systems, in retrospect, I might have taken the trouble to learn a little something about them. She would have sprung for a top of the line security system and it might have been able to protect her, for a little while, from the terrors lurking in the outside world.

But I did nothing towards that end. She drank and talked with me on occasion about various things without ever revealing her emotional core. I respected her intelligence and lucidity. I suppose I was aware of the fact that she was lonesome, but it never occurred to me that she could be so vulnerable.

There is the myth about Southern white women, that they dream of black men as lovers. Whether it is true or even rightly called a myth, it is a truism. Some forbidden longing suppressed in the psyche, perhaps forgotten, for years unacknowledged, surfaces and cannot be denied. A fearful taboo brings forth mystery and new life and changes all that has gone before. To be sure, the likelihood is very small, that I, Peter Foster, yardman extraordinaire, am even remotely qualified to speculate on the psychology of white women. My only observation regards the existence of the myth, or the truism, of the black incubus.

In Voris' case, I suppose some secret wish was being fulfilled. Some thirst for excitement or self-abandonment must have come into play. In the next few months, a single black man, a young, heavyset fellow, began doing all her odd jobs. He'd answer the door when I knocked and tell me Voris wasn't home, or that she was taking a nap and didn't want to be disturbed. Soon, there were several young blacks over there all the time, coming and going at all hours, carrying boxes of merchandise out to their cars.

These were strange goings on.

Clarence would scowl, his sense of outrage undisguised. "What did I tell you?" he said one day as we watched several of them loading Ray Fletcher's fishing poles through the window of a battered green Ford. "Them buzzards'll take everything she's got."

I couldn't believe it was happening. She was writing checks for hundreds of dollars. The ringleader brought in some of his friends and they worked on her until she had drained one account of thirty thousand dollars.

Her next door neighbor, Mr. Willets, had been her husband's closest friend. He had also worked at the bank with Voris, the bank where she still kept her accounts. We had spoken on several occasions before and one day we were both raking and watching the cars come and go at Voris'. We exchanged looks of concern, stopped raking and I crossed the street to talk with him again. He expressed his grave concern at Voris' situation. She had not been seen outside her home in weeks. Her plants had not even been watered.

Mr. Willets did not want to embarrass her but he thought it was time to call the police. "She needs some kind of protection."

Once, in the grocery store, I had followed the ringleader up and down the aisle while he filled his cart with steaks and expensive delicacies. He was bragging to a cohort about the pile of money he was soaking out of Voris. He mentioned cocaine and I had some trouble clearing my mind of a grotesque vision of Voris, cocaine and a house full of black men demanding checks of outlandish proportions.

"I'm going in there," said Mr. Willets. "You coming?"

We rapped on her door with our rake handles. No one answered.

We walked around to the side of the house and saw that all the shades were drawn. When we got to the back, we heard the commotion out front of cars starting up and leaving. We came back around to the front and the cars were gone.

The front door was open. Inside, we found Voris in bed. The room smelled of whiskey, sweat, and something else. An empty liter bottle of Canadian whiskey lay discarded on the dirty brown carpet, inches below a recent dent in the wall.

Voris, looking a hundred years old, her matted gray hair in disarray, peeked out from under the sheets. "Leave me alone," she croaked.

Her house was littered with signs of reckless disregard, drawers emptied, papers and trash strewn in haphazard piles. The only items that appeared untouched were the rows of books on the shelves.

Mr. Willets called an ambulance, which came and took Voris away.

I took it upon myself then to water her plants, clean up and look after her house while she was gone. Maintenance duties reverted to me. The green Ford drove by a few times without stopping. After a week or so, it never returned.

Voris would call me from time to time. She was in the care of HRS, having been adjudicated no longer competent to discharge her own affairs. As no family members were alive to commit her, the source of that judgement was puzzling. By some official ruling, her power of attorney was transferred to the HRS.

A couple of times a night I would pop over to Clarence's to check on him, see if he needed anything. He slept a greater part of the day and at night sometimes, he'd be up and about, shuffling from room to room. If he heard me come in, he would say, "Is that you, Gerald?"

I'd say, no, it was just me, Pete. And he'd say, "Oh."

Chapter Three
Mandingo and Maud or "Can This Be Love?"

And it came to pass in the second month of her sojourn in the HRS facility that Voris Fletcher met and fell in love with a fellow patient in the mental ward, a manic depressive middleaged man thirty years her junior named Henry Goodnight, who, as events would have it, was black.

In the fullness of time, about a month later, they were married, at which time they were both unconditionally released from the care and guidance of the HRS. They moved into Voris' house, and Henry, who, in addition to manic depression suffered from agoraphobia, arranged for the installation of a massive security system, replete with the latest laser gadgetry and computerized video surveillance from every angle of approach. Voris was safe now, though her access to her old friends and acquaintances was immediately curtailed. No visitors were allowed her, but, if I said I had come to visit with Henry, I was made to feel welcome in their home.

"He's my master," Voris would say. "I'm his slave." The girlish smile when she said that made it sound like she was joking. But her house was well tended again, and she did not look unhappy, though the burden of carrying around a portable phone in a knapsack at all times did seem to vex her a little. From any room in the house, Henry might call on that phone and instruct her to fetch him a beer or a sandwich or some vital item like a Phillips head screwdriver.

He was setting up his computer room in the spare bedroom. All through the house were empty boxes in which the various components of his equipment had been delivered.

His master plan was to develop a nationwide audio-visual network.

"With this computer," he said with pride, "I'll be able to play chess with a friend of mine in Detroit."

In time, he did achieve that goal. Then set his sights even higher. He was determined to start a photography business. Thousands more were spent on cameras and video equipment. He hired me to write ad copy for him. He also hired me to paint the porch and the bathroom. And I was back to doing yardwork again, for an unconscionably nominal sum. Meanwhile, he purchased expensive equipment freely with Voris' money.

Sometimes when her eyes met mine I would read supplication in them. Other times she would merely shrug, as if she had no will of her own but to serve her lord and master.

Henry liked to call her Irene. Irene Goodnight. Funny guy, that Henry.

When the work he hired me to do was completed, and he paid me, though not without complaint. Not keen on striking up a close friendship with him, I remained somewhat cool toward him. Then he informed me one day that I was his only friend.

Voris explained. "He doesn't make friends easily, Pete."

After he told me that, I stayed away for awhile. A shortage of friends was never my problem.

On Sunday mornings, I could always count on Walter coming by at the break of day. Sunday was his day off and he'd start drinking at four a.m., his regular time to wake up. By six, he'd have half a fifth under his belt, and he'd hop on his bicycle and pedal over to Clarence's. I was most often on the porch, where the sound of my typing was less likely to disturb Clarence's slumber. Most of the time, I was able to intercept Wally before he started banging on the door.

Walter Wellington was, to be kind, not well. I say that with affection for the young man, an epic alcoholic. Many people, such as myself, drink every day, in moderation, with little or no deleterious effects. That may sound like a textbook example of denial and I am willing to concede that it does. But enough about me. Consider Walter: a young man, thirty-five, working in a gas station. A high school graduate, he served in the Army, was honorably discharged, played drums in a touring rock band for the next six years, traveling to major cities around the country. On the band's first trip to Florida, they broke up. The lead singer married and quit. The rest of the band went their separate ways, or back to Connecticut, where they originated. Walter stayed in Florida, liking the weather. He got a job, lost it. Got another job, lost it. Got another job pumping gas. He moved with his wife, Katie, and their dog, Max, into the neighborhood. At that point, he was thirty-two years old. The best years of his life were not behind him. Even if they were, as he, at his most pathetic, would claim, nothing could justify his total lack of moderation.

Clarence had no use for Walter. If he saw him rolling up the driveway on his bike, he'd make a half-hearted effort to get up from his chair, then he'd sink back with a pained smile on his face and await the inevitable.

"Hiya, Clarence," Walter would shout as if Clarence were deaf, "How's it going, old timer?"

A raised eyebrow or a subtle flick of his thumb was a polite indication to me of Clarence's level of annoyance.

He didn't like Walter coming around. But it was impossible to get Walter to stop coming by. Every Sunday morning, he came wheeling up. Until Clarence was dead and I had to move.

When that happened, I was at a loss. Where to go and what to do were my biggest immediate problems.

Gerald was due to show up from Germany within the week. He was sure to boot me out. In fact, his first and only words to me when he saw my suitcase on the patio, packed and ready, were, "You're leaving post haste, before I call the police." Then he walked past me as if I were already gone.

Voris and Henry let me park my suitcase in their garage for a couple of days, but they weren't interested in having a boarder.

"A couple of days," said Henry, to his only friend.

Clarence was cremated. His son and his daughter stayed around for the reading of the will. His daughter got the house. Gerald got the stock. No one else got anything, not even me, his faithful butler.

Chapter Four
Bingo and Booze, or "It's Not a Pretty Picture."

The tiny garage apartment adjacent to Walter's house was perfect for my purposes, with a desk, chair, lamp, bed and a separate toilet. Walter wanted a hundred and fifty a month, which was reasonable, but made no allowance for my straitened circumstances. I offered him five bucks a day.

"Pete," he said. "I don't know. That doesn't sound so good to me."

At least it wasn't a firm no. I played it cool, left the seed to germinate in his mind. In a day or two, toward the middle of the week, if I were to drop by and lay a few bucks on him, ten or fifteen, say, enough for a pint or two and cigarettes until payday, he might come around, if he could square it with Katie. The problem was the realtor representing the landlord, who, Walter claimed, kept a close eye on the place.

They were renting the house with an option to buy, but until certain papers were signed, the adjacent garage apartment was not theirs to rent and remained vacant at the insistence of the absentee landlady in Arizona.

Katie really wanted that house. She was trying to arrange the financing at reasonable terms. With both of them working full-time, they cleared five or six hundred a week. If she cut back on her bingo nights, and Walter cut back even a fraction on booze, they could handle the payments on the little pink house.

A little rundown, but solid, the house was shaded by a large cedar tree in the front yard. There was a peaceful atmosphere in the old neighborhood, and a fenced back yard for Max. Katie had convinced Walt that they couldn't afford not to buy it. In a couple of years they'd have equity, and it was sure to increase in value once they fixed it up.

The previous landlord, Mrs. Halloran, had lived for years in the house directly behind Walter's on the next street over. Her house was also the same shade of pink, a sort of faded fuchsia.

Mrs. Halloran and her son, Lester, were in separate but equal mental institutions in Arizona, having been committed at length by the daughter, Alberta, the only demonstrably competent member of the Halloran family extant. Alberta was due to inherit her mother's properties, and she was looking to unload them both without delay.

Katie's original agreement was with the realtor representing the elder Mrs. Halloran, however, and whether it would continue to be honored by the daughter was an unknown factor. Insurance investigators had yet to appear on the scene. The Halloran house stood vacant and my little bungalow apartment, already claimed in my mind, also stood vacant, as I moved on down the avenue in the vague direction of Frances' house.

Next door to Walter's stood the Deadbeat Hotel. In a pinch, I always fell back on Floyd. Though he seldom missed an opportunity to remind me of my burdensome nature, and though he preferred living alone, and though he was quick to anger and his manner was often rude toward me, sometimes downright vicious, I never doubted for a moment that we were brothers under the skin. Floyd Tarlton nicknamed his house the Deadbeat Hotel, largely on my account, although I was not, by any true definition, a deadbeat, nor was I the only deadbeat ever to crash on his couch, not by a long shot.

Floyd, the budding novelty songwriter, the next Ray Stevens, was struggling to remain self-employed in the furniture refinishing business. His house was roomier than Walt's, with a miniature room above the garage, hardly bigger than the mattress on the floor. During a previous sojourn there, it was my room, my little upper room.

More than a year had passed since he had ousted me from it. I moved to Clarence's. Plenty of time for his heart to grow fonder of me in my absence.

Floyd and I kidded each other. Not only did he fancy himself the next Ray Stevens but also something of an artist with wood, as well. On either point, he was unresistant to flattery.

With a large dropcloth folded under one arm and a pail containing some tools in the other he came out of the house and spread the dropcloth in the shade of the cedar. Of course, I gave him a hand carrying out the chest he was refinishing down the porch steps and over to the dropcloth in the yard. Never mind my hernia, I was glad to be of help. As long as I avoided sudden movement I was fine.

At that time, I had not yet undergone my second hernia operation. My health was not a problem.

"This is an attractive piece," I said, when we set it down. The big cedar chest had a band of inlaid veneer across the front and sides. The finish, which he was about to remove, was dark and cloudy. Beneath it, lay a thing of beauty; the wood, which he would awaken with his steel wool pads and his attention to detail.

"This jewel is going to look fine," said Floyd.

"I won't disturb the master at work," I said. "I was just in the neighborhood, at Walter's, in fact."

"Wally going to let you move in?" he asked.

"Well, that's in abeyance for now," I said. "The decision is kind of on hold."

"On hold," said Floyd. He began brushing a liberal coat of chemical stripper onto the top of the chest.

"You heard Clarence died."

He nodded. "So, you're out on your ear, eh?"

"Something like that," I said. Sometimes Floyd's sense of humor was a little hard to take.

"Well, I hope you find something, Pete. Maybe Wally will rent you his little room. Maybe Clarence will come back from the dead and let you live there with him awhile longer. Maybe you won't ask me what I know you're going to ask me."

"A couple of days, kid."

"A couple of days," he repeated, looking up at the sky as if he had heard that phrase somewhere before, not looking at me for fear of laughing. I had him.

"I'll mow the lawn. You hate to mow the lawn."

"Pete," he said, "you know, I've really enjoyed this past year with you not living here with me. It's been a pleasure to know you during that time. You come over, you visit, then you leave. I like that." He grinned up at me. "What I don't like is having you around all the time. You got on my nerves pretty bad when you lived here last time, Pete. You made me lose my temper. You made me abuse you verbally, and, of course, you paid no attention to anything I said until I impugned your script, a cheap shot, yes, which I felt guilty for taking, but hey, you can't stand there and tell me we're talking about a couple of days, Pete. Be serious, a couple of days?"

"A couple of days," I said.

"Ok, what's today, Tuesday? Say you're in on Wednesday out on Friday. Is that what you're saying."

"In a literal sense, if you must put it that way."

"What if I refuse? And you take that with the grain of salt to mean maybe, but for no more than two days, or for no more than six months."

"Six months is fine," I said. "Or two days. I want to get into Walter's bungalow. Just hang in there with me for a little while, kid. Just for a couple of days."

"You can't smoke in the house," he said. "You stink up the place something awful."

"Deal." I held out my hand to shake with him. He had on a rubber glove and waved it.

"I have one suitcase and my typewriter over at Voris'" I said, "and my briefcase. If you're going to be home awhile, I'll go get them."

"Yeah, yeah," said Floyd. "Two days, Pete. That's it."

"That's all I need."

That night, when I returned to Floyd's, he had managed to wrestle the chest onto the porch by himself. He sat studying it under the porch light, memorizing the grains and whorls of the wood's character. It was stripped of its finish, and he was fine sanding the final debris from the corners and minute crevices. When he wiped it wet with mineral spirits, the wood revealed a gleaming glimpse of the lustre it would soon acquire. There were imperfections to fill and sand and much buffing yet to be done, but already, the chest was a magnet to the eye.

We were sitting there, silently admiring it, when Walter knocked on the door. Drunk, though not in a state of dementia yet, he pressed his nose to the dirty screen of the porch door. "Hey, boys," he said, "what's happening?"

"You," said Floyd, moving quickly to cover the chest with a cloth as Wally hoisted himself up the porch steps with a tall drink in his hand. He stood tottering as if with vertigo on the porch and observed Floyd over the rim of his glass.

"Katie's at bingo," he announced in the silence. "She's addicted to it." Neither Floyd nor I responded. He went on. "Her problem's worse than mine."

Neither of us asked him to continue his monologue. "Forty, fifty dollars. Forty tops. For a week. That's how much I spend on booze. Forty bucks. A week. You know how many nights a week she goes to bingo?"

"How many, Walter?" I said.

"Lucky seven." He took a big swallow, lit a cigarette. I held up a finger and he tossed me one. "Seven nights a week," he went on. "That's at least twenty bucks a night, unless she wins, which she doesn't. Not that often. One two hundred dollar pot in two years. She breaks even maybe half the time. Still seventy bucks a week. Seventy bucks. A week. On bingo. And she thinks I have a problem."

"You do have a problem," said Floyd.

"Correct," said Walter. "I drink. At least I don't play bingo. If

I played bingo like she does and drank too, man, that would be a problem. I'd have to give one of them up. And I tell you what, it'd be bingo."

"Wally," said Floyd, "are you going to let Pete stay in that bungalow, or what?"

Chapter Five
The Deadbeat Hotel, or Home, Sweet Home

"Who, him?" Walter indicated me. "Nope."

"Why not?" said Floyd.

Walt shook his head, as if the question could only be answered by an economist. "He doesn't have any money," he said. "He doesn't have a dime."

"Yeah, but he means well," said Floyd.

"Perhaps I should retire while you gentlemen discuss my merits."

"No, Pete, don't leave," said Walter.

"I have some important letters to write," I said, "I'll be up half the night at the typewriter. So, if you'll excuse me, Walter." I moved past him into the house. Floyd, seated on the threshold, moved aside to let me pass, but remained in the doorway, blocking Walter's entry.

"Ever seen him type?" said Walter.

Floyd nodded. "Like lightning."

"Lightning," Walt repeated, choking as he drained his glass.

Lucky for me I can take a joke. Turning a deaf ear to what passed for banter between them, I set up my typewriter on the kitchen counter under the light and reeled in a blank sheet of paper. I stared at the white expanse an appropriate length of time, then began to write a letter to a woman named Bess Tillman, who was affiliated in an administrative capacity with Walt Disney Studios in Orlando.

We had spoken on the phone several times and she had read my screenplay and liked it, so I felt comfortable addressing her by her first name. In our last conversation, she had remarked that it seemed like the kind of family oriented film that Disney Studios used to be known for making, and, in her opinion, ought to be making still. But there were changes pending in corporate policy over which she had no control. She could tell me nothing more at the time and our conversation ended on a pleasant, hopeful note.

"Dear Bess," I wrote. As I considered how to continue, my eyes grew tired and the weight of the years since Jenny had left me descended on my head like an imploding building. If I could crawl out from under the rubble that was burying me long enough to show my sons I had not given up, the pride that once was mine might yet be theirs. If I could erase my example in their minds and tell them all I knew and believed to be true in a single word, that word would be the motto of my home state, New York: Excelsior. Ever Upward.

Fine words and mottoes made me tired. I scorned my own pretensions. The effort I made to rise above my surroundings, I saw it clearly for the snobbery it was. I wanted to cease my struggles and sink to the depths, no more to rise, no more to rise above anything or anyone. Shake off the mortal coil and embrace eternal ignominy.

I couldn't go to sleep feeling that low. I took a cigarette and a drink outside and sat on the back steps. Looked at the moon. Thought about Arthur and Bradley, my sons, how they looked at me now was so different than when they were young. In their eyes I could see they no longer believed anything would ever come of my script.

"Don't you have a dream to follow, Dad?" was Bradley's parting shot to me, when he moved in with his older brother. Before he could see how those words hurt me, I left. He didn't mean it.

Arthur knew better what I'd gone through.

Still, I wouldn't mention the Disney thing until I had some good news. Let them believe it when they see it.

The stars shone down on me as I felt the glow of possibilities emanating from afar. I was still in the ring. Still on my feet. I'd just taken an eight count.

THE ROUTE

In the darkness, I renewed my purpose. There was a movie to be made from my screenplay. The distant promise of it still rumbled like a tremor in my bones. I'd come too far to stop believing.

Inside, I had a letter to write. Excelsior.

In the morning, I set out for Mr. Youngblood's. Almost a year ago, I had started painting the outside of his house and he was beginning to drop little hints about the job taking an extraordinary length of time to complete. Not to worry, I told him, used to his good-natured ribbing. The truth was, I'd done a magnificent job on his house and he was pleased in every way with the work. Except for the simple fact that it was not finished, after eleven months, he had no complaints.

My best case scenario for the day was to get a small check from him on account, do a little scraping on the garage door, which was peeling like a nightmare, make a congenial exit and get back to finish it later.

Frances's fence also required my immediate attention. Maybe I could get her to give me a check for the paint. Surely, there was some white paint somewhere in Floyd's garage. No one was ever going to look at her fence, anyway. If I managed to sell her some old paint my conscience wouldn't bother me much. My personal code of ethics was facile enough to wink at that sort of conduct.

As a rule, though, I was scrupulously honest. True, I had long since mastered the knack of rationalizing away minute transgressions, which was a comfort to me in my middle years, having been saddled since childhood with a meddlesome conscience.

A typical boy scout, doing my quota of daily good deeds, as a young man, I was forthright and true, upright in both word and deed, not to mention incredibly handsome, with a voice to melt a young girl's heart and eyes as blue as the sea. My future in the acting profession was, by all accounts, bright, had I stayed in New York. A few moments under the lights garnered notices mentioning me as "a man to watch," all tucked away now in a file somewhere in a trunk, in storage, in Jenny's attic if she still had them. That was for "The Invisible Man," my most memorable performance. The thought never occurred to me then, as my head was being swaddled with pounds of gauze that I would remain invisible for the rest of my life. But I fell in love with a wonderful woman and soon learned that I had fathered a child. She was Canadian. I married her, and moved to Toronto.

I never regretted the move, only the irretrievable loss of momentum. The marriage didn't last. We parted without rancor. I said goodbye to Elise and my young son, Peter, and returned to New York. But I had lost the spark, the single-minded dedication of youth to the art of drama. I couldn't make the commitment again. Besides, I had a job writing radio commercials. And I had met Jenny, the woman who would become my wife and the mother of Arthur and Bradley.

My memories of the next twenty-four years, which we spent together in relative harmony do not condense well. The harshness of our final divorce overshadows, in my mind, the affections that kept us together so long. Were I to attempt a chronology of our marital decline, I am certain insufferable melancholia would be the only net result.

So I scraped Mr. Youngblood's garage door, sanded the rough edges, and filled the crevices with smooth beads of caulk, taking a craftsman's pride in my work. If it took me a full year to paint a house, so be it, when I was done it was a well-painted house.

Mr. Youngblood laid a twenty on me and I promised to finish by the twenty-seventh of June, a year to the day since I started. He seemed satisfied with our arrangement, and somewhat amused. When I left he was standing at the end of his driveway, admiring his garage door.

As I was leaving the liquor store, I ran into Eugene, a homeless person who collected cans and could often be seen pushing a shopping cart piled high with crushed cans, his gaunt frame straining in the heat with his load. Or he might be sipping a cold beer on the shady side of an abandoned building, his bare back pressed against the cool concrete. Warm months, he slept in a bush behind the bowling alley. In winter I think he suffered, but he was never far from his area.

As usual, he had a cheerful word. "Mister Pete," he said with a childlike grin. "Boy, ain't it hot today? I'm about ready for a beer, ain't you?"

"Indeed," I replied, exiting as he approached the door. On any other day, that exchange would have completed our conversation. But he asked me to wait for him. He wanted to ask me something.

When he came out we walked across the parking lot to the place he had cached his cart behind a dumpster. He was watchful, and spoke as if he feared being overheard. "Mister Pete," he said, "most people think I don't have no money. But I got it hid real good. Two bags full."

Why he was confiding in me I had no idea.

"You've always been a friend to me," he said next, as if in answer to my unasked question. "You gave me cigarettes. You gave me a drink before when I needed one." He tapped his temple. "I don't forget. And I want to do something for you now."

"That's kind of you, Eugene," I said, "but it's not necessary."

He handed me a pack of Chesterfields. "This ain't it, Pete. This is extra. What I want to do is give you some money. I got two bags. I'll give you one if you'll help me write my will."

I was grateful for the cigarettes. The rest had come too fast for me to react.

"Just help me," he said, "I had a premonition. In case something happens, I ain't got no folks. But I know you need the money. And before anybody steals it, I rather you to have some."

"You're far too generous, Eugene."

"Pete," he said, "I don't know what to do with it all. Will you help me?"

"Of course."

"Good. I feel better already. You know where to find me?"

"Third bush."

He grinned with simple innocence. "See you later, then. Thanks, Pete." He waved once and pointed his cart down the alley. He was singing an unrecognizable tune.

There, but for the grace of God, went I.

The thought of tackling Frances' picket fence was too daunting that late in the day. Better to start it fresh in the morning. With Eugene's premonition on my mind, I set my steps for home. Home sweet home.

Chapter Six
The Secret of the Pink House or Piano Lust, Part One

A well-traveled path cuts across the barren lot behind the L'il Champ, through a thicket of burrs and sandspurs that cling to shoelaces and cuffs. Eleventh Street is a long straight paved road that runs the length of Gonzalez Park past a playground with swings and picnic tables, a basketball court and baseball diamond, where Little Leaguers and softball teams gather for regular practice. The sandspurs in the outfield sometimes grow as high as my knees before the City gets around to mowing it. Unless I'm in a big hurry, I stick to the pavement.

Down Eleventh Street walking towards me I thought I recognized Lester Halloran. But it was a tall kid, swinging a baseball glove instead of a large Coke bottle. The closer he came, I could see it wasn't Lester, who had an unmistakable way of walking splay-footed, with his toes turned outward at a broad angle. Duck footed, we used to call it. He had big dark eyes, with dark circles around them, the better to stare down the curious few who dared look him in the eye as he took his daily walk to the L'il Champ to buy his large Coke. His hair hung untended in scraggly strands to his shoulders and the jeans and the shirts he always wore were very old. He never wore shoes.

He talked to no one very much. The clerk at the store would

take his empty bottle and he'd pay her for the new one, minus the deposit, and return the way he'd come. He used to live in the shed behind his mother's house. He'd lived there for years. He told me she would no longer let him into the house.

For some reason, he talked to me. I'd walk past his corner and he'd wave me over, or our paths would intersect near the park, and I'd walk along with him awhile. He was perfectly lucid when he wanted to be. Then he'd go off on a tangent regarding alien beings, top secret government files, or spies.

His intelligence, I learned, was once acute. He repaired computers in the Army and was stationed in Germany when his accident occurred. In short, he was electrocuted, the technical equivalent of inserting a screwdriver into a light socket. That it happened at all was a fluke. That he lived was a sardonic twist of fate.

Honorably discharged, the husk of what remained of Lester Halloran came home to live with his mother. He received a disability check every month, but at some point, his mother began cashing his checks and doling him out an allowance of twenty bucks a week, enough, by some standards, to live on. He ate very little. I never saw Lester eat. But his haunting eyes, I remember the earnest bewilderment in them, as if a hint of half-forgotten memories lay close at hand yet somehow out of reach.

"The money," he said. "That's why she won't let me in the house. She's been cashing my checks for five years. There's money hidden all over that house. In books. She doesn't even know where she hides it. She's as bad as me. She doesn't remember."

We were smoking cigarettes in his shed when he told me. He had a little cot and a hotplate, a few little shelves. An extension cord ran into the garage, where there was a sink and a little bathroom.

"If I want to get in the house I can," he said. "She doesn't think I know how."

I'm at my best in situations where a confidence is unsolicited. Never asking the obvious question, I just nod and listen.

"Through the attic," he said. "But it's dirty. Last time I went in

I unlocked a window. She forgets to check the windows."

"The window," I repeated. "Makes sense."

He held up one long finger. "Most of the money," he said, "the CIA doesn't even know where most of the money is, but I know."

I looked at him, neither skeptical nor questioning, and waited.

"In the piano," he said, putting his finger to his lips. "That's where most of it is."

He went on a little more without delineating how the CIA fit into the picture. Then he stopped talking and stared at my cigarettes. I shook out a couple and left them for him.

"I'm swearing you to secrecy," he said.

"Mum's the word, Lester."

"Exactly, Pete," he said, "mum is the word."

Sworn to secrecy, I kept mum. Lester was gone, yet I often thought about the money he claimed was hidden in the Halloran house. Now, as I turned the corner, a fumigation tent covered the entire structure, including Lester's old shed. The contents of that property had yet to be thoroughly inventoried. No small task, that. The inside of the house was rather cluttered.

Mrs. Halloran had hired me on various occasions to mow her yard. Once or twice I had helped her carry in groceries. She'd become forgetful and had long since ceased to use the kitchen cabinets. The groceries were left out and spread within easy reach upon every available surface. Floors, tables, chairs, counters, windowsills; all were being used as storage spaces. Cans of beans, soup, peas, corn, yams and spaghetti sauce were stacked four high on the dining room table. Roaches and fleas had the run of the place.

Mrs. Halloran, somewhere in her eighties, had lost her grip. Later, she would forget to bring the groceries in at all. Walking by, I'd see the brown bags full of rotting food in her stationwagon. When her daughter in Arizona became aware of her condition, she immediately employed the Myers Act. A realtor appeared and locked up the house. Now it was being fumigated and the neighborhood gossip was that both Lester and his mother had been institutionalized in Arizona.

When the dioxin dust settled, insurance appraisers would go over the Halloran house with a fine tooth comb. If they started finding caches of cash in every nook and cranny, they'd be honor bound to report every penny. Somehow, I found it doubtful that their consciences were as dutiful as mine.

As I turned the corner for home, I could hear the confluent sounds of laughter and of Walter stumbling around inside his house, wreaking havoc with breakable things. Floyd had his dropcloth out in the yard again. He was working on a small spice rack. His laugh was still rippling when he waved me over.

"I got Wally good," he said. "He can't find his car keys. He's been tearing up his house all afternoon looking for them. And he came over here awhile ago, looking for you. Maybe he thought you had them. He's totaled."

"Bombed?"

"Oh, yeah. So I'm out here working and I see him come and go. I don't even ask him what he's looking for. Then he comes over to me and says he lost his keys."

"Well, I said, "did you look behind the couch?"

"Yes," he says, "I looked behind the couch."

"Did you look under the couch?"

"Yes, I looked under the couch," he says.

"Did you look in the cushions of the couch?"

"Yes, I looked in the cushions of the couch."

"Did you look on the kitchen table?"

"Yes, I looked on the kitchen table."

"Did you look in the bathroom?"

"Yes, I looked in the bathroom."

"Did you look in the garbage?"

"Yes, I looked in the garbage."

"Did you look inside the refrigerator?"

"He starts to say yes, but then he stops and says, "Fuck you, Floyd, you asshole!" Then he goes into his house again and that's when all the noise started. I don't know what the hell he's breaking in there. Sounds like he smashed up his guitar."

A few hours later, Katie came over to Floyd's with tears in the corners of her eyes. "Wall found his keys," she said. "They fell down behind the dresser. First, he tore the whole house apart. broke everything, dishes, things my mother gave me. I told him, why don't you ever break your own things? So he started breaking his records. He broke a bunch of albums. I don't know what to do. He won't quit drinking. Go to A.A., I told him. It's right up the street. But he won't. I didn't even clean up the mess. I'm not picking it up this time. When he wakes up it'll still be there. I can't even have nice things in the house. As soon as I get something nice, he breaks it."

The least I could do was offer to help Walt straighten things up. If I was ever going to get in that bungalow, I needed her on my side.

"Thanks, Pete," she said. "When he wakes up, tell him I'm at bingo."

Chapter Seven
A Day Late, or A Dollar Short

The next morning, I intended to slip out early without waking Floyd. To keep from coughing I held my breath until my hand was on the knob. The tickle in my throat betrayed me. The door was unlocked already, which meant that Floyd was up and sitting on the front steps with his coffee.

As I eased the porch door open he moved aside to let me squeeze out. Three doves were pecking through the sparse grass by the road. In the quiet their soft coos were most melodious.

"Tomorrow's Saturday, Pete," said Floyd.

So it was.

"Are you going to have somewhere to go?"

"Just like that?"

"A couple of days," he said, like a voice quoting scripture.

I took the seat beside him on the concrete steps.

"You're no closer than you were two days ago to having a place to go. Are you?" He bowed his head, rubbed his eye sockets with his thumbs, as if to relieve unimaginable stress, and sighed, "You're getting ready to do your sandcrab act again."

"Floyd," I said, "I've got something in the mill."

"What, the Disney thing?"

"No. That's in limbo. Not dead, just not a concern at the moment. For them or for me. This is different."

"Here it comes."

"No, hear me out," I said, "you asked. I've been in touch with some important people."

"Yeah?"

"You follow me?"

"Important people?"

"In Miami. Friends of the boys. You follow me?"

"Follow what? Follow where?"

"If you'll just let me tell you."

"Well, then, quit asking do I follow. Just get on with it. Friends of the boys."

"The upshot of it is I've got a straight line to Havana."

"I don't follow you."

"I talked to Castro's brother-in-law on the phone. Tito."

"Yeah? How's he doing?"

"Tito Saenz. You know my Spanish is not too bad. It's as good as his English. I tell you, kid, I'm good on the phone. He's got the Bank of Havana at his fingertips and I've got what, eight cents in my pocket and a script he hasn't even read yet, and we're talking about making a movie. We're talking venture capital, independent production, the whole bit."

"Tito and Pete?"

"Serious bread. He's a Cabinet minister. Director of Propaganda, something like. He made a couple of documentaries about the military, now he wants to make movies. Maybe he just wants to bury some money. Maybe he wants to take a bundle out of Cuba while he has the chance. The dough's burning a hole in his pocket."

"Tito and Pete?"

"Something like that. You think I'm kidding?"

He couldn't keep the smirk off his face. "Why would Tito fund an independent production? No offense, but can't he find a safer investment?"

"Because he's got the bug, kid. Those Latins love Hollywood."

"Pete," said Floyd, "that's the most ridiculous thing I ever heard."

"It's true," I said.

"So you're going to get back with Tito on that."

I shrugged. "We're going to make a movie, kid."

Leave them laughing when you can. Floyd tried to keep a stone face. But he was no Jack Benny.

"Heard from Guntar Godor lately?" he asked, a sly reference to a former business acquaintance of mine, who, like Tito, also had a yen to invest in the movie business. He was a wealthy German philanthropist and something of a great white hunter, as well, who went to Kenya twice a year to hunt big game. He had promised to get back with me when he returned from Kenya, but my phone was disconnected by then and if he ever did call back, I missed the call.

"Guntar's fine," I said. "He called the other day. He's back from Africa and living in Neptune Beach. With his mother, the Queen of Spain."

So much for Jack Benny. "Listen," I said. "I've got a hundred and sixty-seven pickets to scrape at Frances' house. Do you have any white paint?"

He said he would check the garage later. I gathered up my little sack of tools, my paint scraper and scraps of sandpaper, and headed up the road.

To scrape one picket takes longer than it does to paint it. Right away I knew I should have charged her by the hour. The day grew hot so fast. By mid-morning, I was ready to pass out from heat exhaustion. Fourteen pickets were scraped on both sides, and fourteen more on one side only. The kudzu vine that had formed an unnatural bond with part of the fence also had to be clipped back. I was dizzy with the mathematics of my task. Numbers were pinging in my head like a pinball counter. two hours to scrape fourteen pickets, that was basically seven pickets an hour. A hundred and sixty-seven divided by seven was almost twenty-four hours worth of scraping. Dividing that into the fifty bucks, I had agreed to scrape and paint the fence for somewhere around a dollar an hour, with a built-in risk factor of possibly not being paid. The worst part of it was knowing I couldn't do it any faster.

Unless I skipped the scraping. I was already skipping the priming. What difference would it make to Frances? She wasn't about to come outside and look. She'd never get closer to that fence than the front porch, and it would look fine from there, nice and white. Maybe I'd just scrape the front side, or maybe have a little talk with Frances about working by the hour.

I decided it was best to be up front with her about the money. I took a break, went inside to get a drink of water, and sat down across a table with her on the porch where she'd been sitting, watching me work.

"Is it hot out there, Pete, or what?" she said.

"Frances," I said, "really, fifty bucks, you know, the kind of work I'm doing, the scraping, that fence has never been scraped, the sanding, fine meticulous preparation, as it should be done, you understand, and nothing would give me greater pleasure than to continue doing it that way, so it's done right, but you know, on an hourly basis, you'd be much more likely to get that optimal result. This way, for fifty bucks, I can't afford to scrape it the way it should be done."

"Can't afford to scrape it?" Frances said. "You can't afford not to scrape it."

My best response was no response.

"You're not going to paint it? Ok, don't."

"Frances, with all the scraping involved I would rather start from the beginning at an hourly rate. That way, I can pick away at it, and you won't have to pay the whole amount out at once."

"When you going to be done?"

"Don't worry about that," I said.

"When?" she pressed like a lawyer. "When will you be done?"

"First, I need some money to buy the paint with."

"How much?"

"Fifteen dollars ought to do it."

"Where do you buy your paint?"

There had to be a snag. "At the paint store."

"Where else do they sell paint?"

My hopes were sinking. "K-Mart, Ace Hardware."

"Mildred works at Ace Hardware. I'll get her to pick up some for me. What kind did you say to get?"

"Frances," I said, "I can probably get some cheaper than even Mildred can with her employee discount. A good friend of mine is in the paint business. He might be able to pick up some very good paint for you at an excellent price."

"You wouldn't overcharge me on the paint, would you, Pete?"

If I had any dignity left, I would have walked away then.

"Oh, I didn't mean nothing by it. Pete, you ought to know me better than that. Just funnin', you old sourpuss. Let me ask you this?" She paused for a moment. "Did I ever tell you to scrape that damn fence?"

"As a matter of fact," I said, " you never did, in so many words, mention scraping. For some reason I assumed that because it should be scraped prior to painting, you would want it to be scraped. As a general rule, when a fence is in that kind of shape, it takes a fair bit of work to put it right."

"Don't matter to me if it's scraped or not. I just want it painted. You can tear it down and make firewood out of it, all I care. Long as you're hanging around looking for something to do you might as well keep busy. Hell, just paint the damn thing and get it over with."

"Frances," I said, "let me have a piece of paper." She found a pencil nub and a napkin for me and I totaled up my figures: two and a half hours at three-eight-five an hour came to about nine dollars and sixty-two cents. If she would part with a ten spot for the time I had in on it already, and another ten for the paint, I told her I would come back every day until the job was done.

"If it takes you a week or a year and a week, you won't get a penny more than fifty bucks."

"Fair enough."

We shook hands on it. "You think you're slick," she said. "But I seen you coming."

I didn't have to ask her what she meant. She was surely going to tell me."

"Ten dollars." She held up a ten for me to look at while she spoke. "I want two coats of paint on that fence. You don't have to scrape it, but I want it to look nice. And I ain't buying no paint from you till you bring it here and let me look at it. Mildred will get me some good paint. I don't want no old paint that's been sitting too long. That's no damn good. Get me some good paint." She finally held the ten out to me. My hand closed on it and I stood up to leave.

"There you go again," she said. "What's your hurry, mister?"

"Frances," I said, "is there something else I can do for you?."

"How about picking me up a liter and bringing it back by? Would you mind?"

"Certainly, Frances, but I'm leaving right now, and I have several other important matters to attend to. It might be a couple of hours before I make it back."

"Never mind, then. I ain't out yet, I guess. Go on, don't let the screen door hit you in the ass on your way out."

Frances' friend from Ace Hardware, Mildred, pulled up in the driveway as I stepped off the porch. She had several bags of groceries for Frances and I helped her carry them in. She seemed very subdued.

"You look a little pale, Mildred, I said. Are you feeling all right?"

"Pete, the strangest thing happened," she said. "A man keeled over and died in the parking lot. Had a heart attack right there. He was that man, I know you've seen him. He's been around forever, what was his name? He collected cans."

"Eugene?"

"That's him," she said. "He had a heart attack and died in front of the grocery store."

News can seem so remote when it comes second or third hand. I was going to find time to help him write his will.

"And when the police came," she began.

"Eugene?"

"And when the police came, they went through his things that were all in his cart. Down under the cans, you know what they found?"

"Money?" I guessed. A wild guess.

"Two thousand dollars. Two socks full, down under the cans. Isn't that weird? He was a homeless."

As I walked down the street away from Frances' with Eugene's will a day late in my mind, I felt in my shirt pocket for cigarettes. The crumpled pack that Eugene had given me less than twenty-four hours earlier had one last Chesterfield in it. I needed a drink and something to eat. I added cigarettes to my mental shopping list, but when I rang up the total, I was about a dollar short.

Chapter Eight
My Three Sons, or Blues for a Family

A powerful need to see my sons came over me as I headed homeward.
Arthur worked nights as a chef in one of the finer restaurants. There was little chance of Bradley being home. Bradley didn't hang around the hive.

There was a woven motto hanging on Bradley's bedroom wall: THE BEE THAT GETS THE HONEY DOESN'T HANG AROUND THE HIVE.

Not what I would call words to live by, but it suited Brad. He was a young hound, lifeguarding at the beach, so drop dead handsome it hurt to look at him sometimes, knowing he was so much like me, and so much like his brother, Peter.

The phones started ringing for Bradley when he was twelve years old. They kept on ringing, young girls calling for Brad. He was a gifted child, born to charm. Clever and quick, and he could be so cruel.

We were close when he was young. He overcame an early affliction with polio, and thereafter considered himself invincible.

Did he break hearts? Do young girls cry? Does a father always think he knows the answer?

I never saw action like that in my teens. There were nods, at least, to the rules of courtship in my day. The world turned. I was hep to all that. Anyway, Bradley stopped listening to me a long time ago.

Arthur's apartment had a strong metal door. No sounds emanated from within. Thinking he might be gone or napping, I started to turn away after a light double knock he would have recognized as mine were he up and about inside. The door opened.

"Arthur," I said his name.

"Hi, Dad." He paused a second longer than he might have meant to before inviting me in. Unmindful, though not unaware of the hesitation, I was so happy to see him, he could have insulted me and I would not have minded.

We sat down and talked. Jenny kept in touch with Arthur. My name, he feared, would nevermore cross her lips. Hers seldom crossed mine either anymore, and it was just as well. We were well and truly finished.

Arthur and Bradley had both been treated to Jenny's side of our story. Mine was private, not for competition.

Arthur was off from work that night. Bradley was away with some friends in Daytona and Arthur had planned to watch a couple of video movies alone. Instead, we watched them together. When the late show came on, a horror classic, we watched that, too.

The black and white late fifties texture looked familiar.

"Wait a minute, what's the name of this movie?" I looked around for the listing. Arthur was way ahead of me, with the paper in his hand.

"*The Brain That Wouldn't Die.*"

"*The Brain That Wouldn't Die?*" I said. "Isn't it '*The Thing That Wouldn't Die?*'"

"Says here '*The Brain That Wouldn't Die.*'"

"They must've changed the title," I said, "I think I'm in this movie!"

"I thought this was the one," said Arthur.

"There's a beauty contest coming up," I said. "Unless they cut me out of the picture, I introduce the girls. Wait a minute, the lines are coming back to me, 'Backstage are five of the girls who have reached the contest finals and we are here to choose Miss Body Beautiful. Now, we have eliminated every one except the five finalists and they will be judged solely by your applause. So let's bring them on.' One by one I introduce the girls, but only four come out. Can you get this on video?"

Arthur said he'd search it out. There was another horror movie, '*The Brides Wore Blood*.' I was the demon ghoul in that one.

My scene came up and was over so fast. For a few short seconds I was walking across that ancient stage again as a young man with a young man's grace and style, giving a fair reading to my lines, such as they were, but they had cut so much out of my scene.

A typical B film in those days might cost a hundred thousand to make. '*The Brides Wore Blood*' was made for thirty thousand. We filmed it in St. Augustine for peanuts."

Arthur had often heard me dissemble on the history of low-budget films. I was a walking compendium of cinematic trivia. Arthur let me ramble through the story again about the films I made with Lee Jennings, the Director and Producer of "*Muddy Mama*," and "*The Brides Wore Blood*," who was so confused by the so-called "plot" of "*The Brides Wore Blood*," which he had created by pirating every cliché from every horror film on record and stirring them all together in a gothic mishmosh, about a young woman, impregnated by a vampire, in a quandary over whether or not her child would inherit the family curse. He came to me at the end and said, "Pete, how the hell do I get out of this thing? You're a writer. Give me an ending."

My fee to be the ghoul was a hundred bucks. He knew better than to offer a writing credit as I had no intention of claiming any part of that script as my own. For twenty bucks I went into the trailer with him and hashed it out. I contributed one line to the film, the last line.

There is a gypsy woman, an old fortuneteller with a Slavic accent, who, in a scene with the aged Count DeLorca, a white haired gentleman with a thin gypsy mustache, consults a huge dictionary, which is supposed to be a secret volume in an occult library. With grave dignity, she closes the book and the pages slap together. The soundtrack is so bad, in that solemn moment, it sounds like an immense breaking of wind.

"Good news," she says, "the child will be born normal."

They hurry to the attic room where the expectant mother is being kept to inform her of the happy news only to find she has broken a mirror and stabbed herself in the stomach with a jagged shard.

Hence the title.

"I'll keep an eye peeled for that one," said Arthur.

Arthur's dry sense of humor was like Jenny's. He had her intellect, her gift for understatement. I hoped he never turned bitter toward me. I wasn't sure I could endure it if he did.

My brilliant son, Arthur, who had earned scholarships in science and music, was professorial material by nature and disposition, but his college days had been short and few and far behind him now, because I had failed to provide him with the wherewithal to continue his education once the scholarships ran out. I would have torn my heart out for him. But I couldn't keep him in college.

"How's the script going, Dad?" he said.

"It might need another rewrite."

He shook his head. "I never know if you're joking or not when you say things like that."

"I'm joking. The script is tight."

"It was tight ten years ago."

"Much tighter now."

"Any news?"

"Spoke to Caminiti again. He'll be in touch."

"Timing is everything," said Arthur, snatching my next line. He knew my friend, Rico Caminiti, was working his Las Vegas connections on my behalf to secure funding for an independent production. Old news. Rico was a showman, a horn player, bandleader and comedian. An entertainer's entertainer, he worked all the time and knew everyone in Las Vegas. I had a fabulous part for him in the script. He wanted to see that movie made almost as much as I did. Still, it took time.

"Do you remember when Peter came down?" I said.

"No, Dad, I was only fifteen. My memory was not fully formed yet."

"Sometimes it's too much for me to think about that day. I'm glad you were home tonight."

The memory of Peter, my son, ten years ago, when he came down from Canada on his vacation, ran through my mind like a flickering home movie captured on soundless 8mm film.

He drove down with his girl in a white Toronado. Elise, who was spotty about keeping in touch, had written that he was coming. In the summer of his twentieth year he was coming to meet his father and his brothers for the first time.

The four of us were living at Bennett's Beach Motel in a bungalow apartment. We were looking for a better place, but we were all together, at least. That mattered. When Peter arrived, he was received by a family who loved him.

His face was my face, his shoulders, my shoulders. His eyes, Elise's eyes, were warm and wet with joyful tears. "Dad," he said. We shook hands and hugged.

At the pool that afternoon, he taught Bradley how to dive. I watched his back flip, admiring his lithe coordination and the physical confidence he projected. Bradley was only eleven, but in Peter he could see himself as he wanted to be, and as he would be. Arthur, my shy and thoughtful one, sat apart in the shade of a poolside umbrella during the diving lesson, reading a magazine, until Peter came over and splashed water on him, saying, "Hey, get wet, little brother."

In the time it took Arthur to smile, Peter had won his heart, too. He jumped in the pool and played like the little brother he had never been before.

Jenny held my hand as we watched our boys with their long lost brother. "Oh, happy day," she whispered to me. I had no words to thank her.

Peter and Janet, his girl, announced at dinner that they were heading south in the morning to Daytona for the races and then they would stop back by before they headed for home. A week later they were back. "Too soon," they said, too soon their vacation was over.

We had dinner with them again before they had to leave.

During the long, teary goodbye, the lump in my throat would not go down. We all stood waving at them from the curb as they pulled out of that driveway and out of our lives. We were together then, a family. And we were together when the phone rang, two days later, with the news of the highway accident that had claimed both their lives.

Bill, Elise's husband called. I turned to the wall when I heard. When I looked at my family again, their eyes were all on me. Then and there I had to tell them what had happened.

A freak accident. A statistic. A gift of love and life given and taken away so fast. A sudden, permanent bruise in my heart. I had to say something. One look at Jenny and somehow she knew. I went to the cabinet and poured a drink.

"What is it, Dad?" said Arthur. "Is it about Peter?"

I couldn't look at Bradley without seeing Peter as a child. Keeping eye contact with Arthur steadied me. "Peter had an accident in his car," I said. "He and Janet were both injured fatally."

Arthur put his arm around Bradley, whose eyes were welling with tears. I went to them both and held them and Jenny spread her arms around the three of us and we all held on to each other and wept. For Peter. For Janet. For ourselves. For each other. For our family.

That was the last time I ever saw Bradley cry.

Chapter Nine
The Make Do Band, or Neighborhood Tunes

In the dead hour before dawn, I headed back to Floyd's, refreshed by an hour's nap on Arthur's couch, leery, even in the best of times, of overstaying my welcome there.

My cigarette trailed a lone red glow in the suburban darkness. One with the stillness and silence of night, the only sounds besides my footsteps were the armies of moths thumping against the luminous glass globes of streetlamps casting lambent patterns of regularity down the length of Tenth Street.

In Voris' yard, another cigarette glowed in the shadows by the concrete bench near the fence. I cleared my throat to alert the smoker of my approach and the cigarette disappeared, but a house slipper dangled from the toe of a crossed leg at the shadow's edge. I heard my name whispered and cleared my throat again.

Voris ventured partway into the light and waved me toward the grotto like juncture of the front and side fences where the foliage thickened and the shadows were deepest. With a hand on the padlocked gatepost, I watched her retreat into the darkness, flicking her lighter until it lit.

"We should stop meeting like this," I said.

"Hey, Pete," she said. "I can't sleep. What's your excuse? A late date?"

"Actually, Voris, I couldn't sleep either. I was with Arthur, thought I'd take a walk. Nice night for a walk."

She pulled her pink bathrobe close to her neck. "A little chilly," she said. "You look like a ghost walking down that road, Pete. All skin and bones. You haven't been eating right."

At six foot, my ideal weight was one-eighty. For the last several years, I'd been hovering around one-fifty on the scale. Lately, I was down around one-forty, which was a little worrisome.

"I'll cook you dinner," she said, "come over tonight. Henry wants to see you, too. He's got a new toy, a pool table. He needs someone to play with. You play pool, don't you?"

"Well, not often."

"Oh, Pete," she sighed, "just come to dinner. You don't come around, anymore."

"Voris, it's only been a couple of days since I mowed your lawn."

"Well, I miss talking to you. Pete, I don't have any friends anymore. What have I got myself into?"

"Voris, I don't know what to tell you."

"I know. I married the damn fool. I must be nuts, too."

"Don't be too hard on yourself. He hasn't hurt you, has he?"

"No, he's good to me as long as he's got spending money. When it's gone, I wonder what he'll do."

"Voris. Take control," I said. "For your own sake, take control of your life."

She seemed to wither in the shadows. "What can I do, Pete? He's my master. I can't go against him."

"I don't know what to tell you, Voris," I repeated.

"Just come to dinner, Pete. We both miss you."

"What time?"

"Anytime. Come early."

"Around five?"

"That's fine. I better go in," she said. "Henry might be trying to call me and I left the phone in the house. He won't like that."

The sky was streaking with shafts of early light. An oceanic scent carried on the dawn breeze gave a salty tang to the flavor of the morning. Another Chamber of Commerce day.

I eased into Floyd's kitchen through the side door. That he'd left it unlocked was a good sign. Maybe he'd given a second thought to that ultimatum business.

When Floyd got up I was at the kitchen counter, making a list of things to do. I had an iron or two for the fire. Cash flow was the immediate problem.

"Morning," Floyd murmured, as he heated water on the stove for coffee. "You going to mow the lawn today?"

"The front? Sure, I'll get the front."

"How about the back?"

Mowing Floyd's yard for free was hardly a lucrative pursuit. "The pine cones need to be picked up first. You don't want to ruin the blades."

"Just run over them. That's what I do."

"That's not good for the machine."

"Pick them up, then. You're going to do that today, right?"

"Today or tomorrow."

"Or sometime," said Floyd. He stirred his instant coffee and grinned at me. He seemed to have woken up on the right side of the bed that day. Before that first cup of coffee, it was not often easy to tell. He could turn a gentle ribbing into a snarling slash if his morning mood was viperish. That day he was jolly, a regular Mr. Tambo.

"Or someday."

"Or someday," he repeated. "Someday the back yard will have been mown by you."

"That is correct, sir."

"Well then," he said, "let that be that."

I saluted him, "Will do, Commander."

He heated the water again for a second cup. "Did you hear about Wally getting fired?"

"When, yesterday?"

"They sent him home yesterday morning. Told him he could come back if he went through detox."

Walter wasn't ready for that.

Floyd shook his head. "I don't see the likelihood."

Moments after his name was mentioned, Walter came knocking at the front door. With a drink in one hand and a guitar in the other, he knocked on the glass panel with his forehead.

Floyd unlocked the door. "Not seeing the likelihood," he said, over his shoulder. "Look at him. It's not even eight o'clock."

Walter stumbled in, rattling the ice in his mug and staggering.

Of all the drunks in all the gin joints in all the world, I'd never met one to compare with Walter Wellington in his glory for sheer obnoxious dementia.

"I guess you heard, Pete, I quit my job"

"I heard you got fired. Walter, what's Katie going to do? She can't pay all the bills."

"I didn't get fired. I quit. Adios, pistachios, that's what I told him. See you in the funny papers, boojums. Hey, you're talking to Walter Wellington here, not some nobody."

In earlier days, Walter had been a professional drummer. A trained and talented musician, he was able to read and write music and play a number of instruments. Outside a musical setting, however, his little light refused to shine. And in the last few years, whiskey had all but eclipsed his love of music.

"You want to play some music, Wally?" said Floyd, eyeing the guitar.

"No, I want to play chess."

"Good, because we're all into chess here, every waking moment. As a matter of fact, I'm writing a song about chess, called, 'Baby, don't make me play no more chess.'"

"Let's hear it," said Walter.

"You just did. Can you play it on the guitar?"

"What are the chords?"

"You tell me, you're the guitar player."

"I'm a drummer, not a guitar player."

Floyd had the patience to keep reaching for the musician dormant inside of Walter. For whatever reason, it was a thing to behold.

THE ROUTE

"Wally, when you hold that guitar in your hands and pretend to play it, I tell you, bud, it sounds like you have magic fingers. So pick up your doggone guitar and play. Just like yesterday."

Walter set his drink aside and reached for the guitar. "Pick up my doggone guitar and play," he repeated, strumming aimlessly, "just like yesterday."

Coming from a jazz background, I was no stranger to impromptu gigs. The three of us had fooled around a number of times with some tunes. Floyd was partial to jug band music and collected makeshift instruments like washboards, kazoos, and maracas. Walter played a basic rhythm guitar. I was a jazz drummer, reduced to using paint brushes on a portable typewriter case, with a couple of pots and pans for cymbals.

Any other time, I would sit in with the Make Do Band. Floyd was becoming a rather prolific amateur songwriter. He was tempted to get serious about developing his songs but remained dependent on Walter to provide a semblance of accompaniment. Every session, no matter how unfocused, was recorded. The tapes were good for laughs and helped them both improve the songs. But they had miles and miles to go before they were anywhere at all.

Walter's drinking pattern allowed for a brief window of opportunity during which his attention might focus on recording. No more than an hour of useful time could be gleaned from any session with Walter. In my view, the window was already closed. There was little chance of him making anything but a nuisance of himself that day. Besides, I had to get back to Frances' fence before it got too hot to work.

"There's some white paint for you on the porch by the door," said Floyd.

When I left, Floyd was taping a maraca to Walter's strumming hand.

Chapter Ten
The White Picket Fence, or The Black Cat

A tune popped into my mind that morning, a walking rhythm, kind of slow and easy with a little bounce every second step.

> *It's a tiny little town*
> *With no downtown*
> *Just south of the Georgia line*

If I could still whistle, I thought, running my tongue over the broken stumps that remained of my teeth, I'd be the envy of every bird.

The half-full gallon can of white paint swung in time as I walked to Frances' house, which was, in actuality, Delbert's house, although somewhere along the line, Frances had taken it over. A black cat watched me passing by from underneath a hedge. Glittering yellow eyes followed my steps and reminded me of the story of Delbert's black cat.

Delbert Vernon lived in that house for many years with his wife, whom I never had the pleasure of meeting. Delbert, I met at the liquor store one day when he was stocking up on supplies and loading them into the basket of his tricycle. 'Senior citizen vehicle' was the proper name for it. Upon learning that I was willing to do lawnwork and other odd jobs, he invited me to join him at his house for a drink and maybe to give him an estimate on some yardwork.

Always ready to follow up a lead, I walked the mile to the address he had scrawled on a matchbook cover, and there it was. Set back from the road a few feet further than the houses on either side, was a cottage being reclaimed by the wilderness. The rain gutters across the front, clotted with decades of humus and oak leaves, had split apart at the joints and hung dangerously askew, supported with threads of fishing wire. Vines and undergrowth were strangling the bushes. Weeds in the front yard were up to my neck.

Assaulted by the odor of cats, I knocked on the door. "Come on in," said Delbert. As I crossed the porch and stepped inside, thirty cats froze in place in the living room, every evil eye on me, and hissed like wild animals.

Delbert waved a hand at them, grunted a command to scat and they scattered. "Have a seat," he said. "Want a drink?"

We had a drink and a pleasant chat. In short order I learned that he was a retired chief in the Navy, widowed, that he hated and feared all cats, and that his final decline into a state of incompetency was already well underway.

"This place is kind of rundown," he said. "I used to keep it up, but I don't give a shit anymore. Cats shit everywhere."

There was a picture torn from a magazine tacked on his wall above the television. His eyes kept returning to it, a picture of a black cat with green eyes and a discomforting stare.

"She did it," Delbert said, "She brought those cats here. They're not my cats."

He started hyperventilating and covered his face with his hands. "Please, mister," he shouted, pulling his wallet out of his back pocket, "Get rid of these goddamn cats!" Then he threw his wallet on the floor like he was spiking a football. "I'll give you a hundred dollars." When I failed to react, he picked up his wallet and spiked it again. This time twenties and tens fell out of it. He picked it up again and shook all of the money out. "I don't give a shit," he said, as the bills showered down to the dusty floor. I sat still while he collapsed in his chair and closed his eyes. "Goddamn cats," he muttered. In a few minutes, he was snoring.

Delbert had just cashed his pension check. There were hundreds of dollars on the floor in twenties and tens. I picked up a hundred dollars, and started rounding up the cats.

The first thing I had to do was move the cat food outside. Then I boarded up the hole in the porch door screen. Any other ways they had of getting in I would find in time. I swept the place out, the kitchen first, then the back porch. It was a big job, worth every cent of that first hundred.

When Delbert woke up, he seemed to take my presence for granted. "You can sleep in that room," he said. "There's a cot in there."

Living there was no picnic. As I picked away at the work, which was beyond any hope of completion, I had my typewriter set up on the back porch. The arrangement was manageable, albeit bizarre. Delbert didn't mind having me around. I wasn't aware at the time that he had a girlfriend.

Every day he'd take off on his tricycle. He never told me where he was going and I never asked. Then one day a taxi pulled up in the front yard. The driver got out of the cab and opened the back door and the largest woman I'd ever seen outside a circus squeezed out of the cab.

Her name was Frances. She introduced herself and looked me up and down. She had a soft face, with features that had hardened. My guess was that she was once an attractive woman of normal size.

"You're a tall drink of water," she said.

"A pleasure to meet you, Frances."

She eyed my deck shoes, threadbare and scuffed, my socks, burr laden, my tanned knobby knees, my shorts, an old pair of Arthur's, my shirt, a knit polo style, rather sporting, and rested her inspection on the bridge of my eyeglasses, held together with glue and a piece of adhesive tape.

"What's your business with Mr. Delbert?" she said.

"My business with Delbert," I said, "is a matter of yardwork, odd jobs, and some painting he is considering."

"He said you could live here?"

"He hasn't asked me to leave. My work on this house has been considerable, although far from complete, as you can see."

"I've been here before," she said. "I can see you did some work around here."

"I got rid of the cats."

"That's another thing. What did you do with them?"

"They're around. I haven't let them in the house."

"Have you been feeding them?"

"Of course," I said. "Outside, in the far corner of the back yard. They're wild, Frances, they'll live."

"Where's the black one?"

"I haven't seen the black one."

"He wants the black one. He thinks it's his wife."

"I have no idea where any of them are. I put the food out. They wait till I'm gone to eat it. I don't see them."

"But you hear them, don't you?" she said, with a laugh.

Thirty cats? Yeah, I heard them. "His wife?" I said.

Her smile went smug. "You don't know about his wife, do you?"

"Just that she died some time ago. From what I gathered, three or four years back."

"Four. She died while Delbert was in jail, right here in this house, in that bedroom where you sleep, although, I don't see how in the hell you can sleep in there. She died of pleurisy and pneumonia while Delbert was in jail for drunk. Nothing serious. He was drinking, got in a fight, and they held him for three days. He called the house from jail and Judy didn't answer. He tried to get the law to stop by, but they didn't. He come home to find her three days dead and a black cat sitting on her chest."

"That black cat," she said, "ain't even the same one. He thinks it is. He thinks his wife's spirit is in the black cat. That's why he keeps this damn picture hung up." Her lip curled at the sight of the black cat picture. "I told him to take the sonofabitch down," she said, as she ripped it off the nail and crumpled it up in her hammy fist. "By God, he's a fruitcake."

She tossed the crumpled paper on the floor and looked at me. "What do you think about that, eh?" she said. "You ever hear anything so crazy?"

"Not this week," I admitted.

"And I'm that nut's fiancee. What do you think of that?"

"I might have guessed. Congratulations."

"No offense, but I'm wondering if you're worth keeping around. You look a little puny. I could fatten you up."

"You needn't trouble yourself," I said, "I'll be leaving."

"I don't mean live here," she said. "I'm going to be living here. But you can still work, can't you?"

"Certainly."

"Thing is, I just don't know yet if I can trust you. When I make up my mind, I'll let you know."

On that note, I was dismissed. I didn't stick around to see which one of them would shove the other over the threshold.

'Knock on any door.' That was my philosophy. The people whose lives I entered took me at face value. I was not expected to play any major roles in their lives. If I affected them at all, it was in small ways.

In time, Frances came to rely on me. Whether she trusted me or not depended on her mood. She collected the phone numbers of various people I knew, where I might happen to be and she would track me down if she wanted me for something.

Once she called me in a panic. I was with a writer friend of mine, Larry Graham, at his house. He lived nearby. Larry was a press correspondent during the Vietnam War and had a thousand page novel about his experiences in the black market that no publisher wanted to touch. So he was rewriting it, for the twenty-second time.

He liked to put on a superior attitude about me drinking, as if he didn't remember the weekend he spent hiding from his bride-to-be at my house, forty-eight hours dead drunk in a chair. That was only once. As for him being such a writer, well, I read his book, the first thousand pages of it. I just wondered how much more there was to say about a subject so well covered. He had a different slant on the war. Fine.

Larry was like a brother to me, but his hypocrisy was annoying. He derided my brand of vodka, Dark Eyes, said it was rotting my brain. I felt like telling him to fuck himself, but I didn't have time to tell him how, because the phone rang. Frances needed me right away. She sent a cab to get me.

Without further ado, I left Larry stewing in his superior juices. The cab took me to Frances'. The driver said she'd told him to wait.

"Find Mr. Delbert, please, Pete," Frances pleaded. "He's gone off with his whole check, eight hundred dollars. He'll be drunk, for sure and there's no telling where he is by now. Oh, find him, Pete. Find him before he hurts himself, or throws his damn wallet down the sewer."

The situation came rapidly into focus. With remarkable savoir-faire, I assured her that I would indeed bring Delbert home and obtained from her within minutes a short list of the bars he used to frequent. At the top of the list was Ocean Liquors. The cab took me there first.

Delbert had been there and acquired some pals. A family of tourists in a green van with Arkansas plates had taken him off to some motel to have a party. The bartender, a helpful young woman, said the strangers had seen Delbert's money. He didn't try to hide it. The motel would be close by, she said, because the young girl was walking when she left before the others.

Pointed in the right direction by a bartender who would never know how helpful she was, the cab cruised the beachfront motels for a few blocks until I spotted a green van with Arkansas plates parked in front of a motel door. The driver pulled close and kept the cab running.

The bartender said there were five of them, Grandma and Grampa, a younger couple and a teenage girl. Whether or not they were the kind of people who might be intimidated by an actor, I was going in to get Delbert.

I pounded on the door and heard laughter inside cut short. A man's voice said, "Who is it?"

"Here for Delbert," I barked.

"Who?"

I pounded harder. "Open up."

The door opened. A blonde Appalachian princess with a prominent cleft palate peeked through the opening.

"Excuse me," I said, pushing the door wide. She wore a patterned pajama top over her bathing suit. Beyond her, between the beds, Delbert sat on the floor in his underwear, watching the television.

"Hey, Pete," he said, "what are you doing here?"

"I came to get you, Delbert. Where are your pants?"

At the kitchenette table, sat an old couple playing cards. They looked up once and went on with their game.

"Johnny and Mama went out," said the girl. I don't know when they'll be back. You can take him with you," she said, indicating Delbert with some distaste.

"Where are his pants?"

"I don't know, Mister."

"You better find them before I call the police." Delbert was staring at the television again.

"Hold on there," said the old man. "He took his own pants off. No one took them off him. We ain't had but a few beers with him." The girl pulled the pants out from under the bed. "Here they are," she said, "right where he left them."

The wallet was in them, empty. "About eight hundred bucks light," I said to the old man as I stepped to the phone, fully intending to call the police. The local gendarmerie, of course, would do nothing to retrieve Delbert's money for him, but the tourist family wanted no trouble with the law.

"Johnny's going to be pissed," said the old woman.

"Here," the old man handed me a roll of folded bills. "That's all he had left. I was just holding it for him till he sobered up. A man like that shouldn't be let out. He's just looking for trouble. Go on, get him out of here. I'm tired of looking at him."

Delbert managed to put his pants on and allowed me to maneuver him into the cab. The bill count was somewhere around five hundred dollars. I pocketed the overage, some thirty bucks, restuffed his wallet and gave it to Frances. She counted the money, then fussed over Delbert for a minute. He turned on the television, took his pants off, and sank into his chair with a beer.

Frances gave the cabbie fifty bucks. Gave me twenty. "Thanks, Pete," she said, "I knew I could count on you."

Who else could she count on? Who else was going to paint her picket fence white?

Chapter Eleven
The Worst Band in the World,
or Meet The Rubes

Frances gave me six bucks for the paint. She loved to haggle and knew it just made me tired. The paint was worth at least ten.

While I put in a good half day on the pickets, she sat fanning herself on the back porch with a tall pitcher of ice water and a liter of bourbon on the table in front of her and a little fan set up in the doorway to blow cool air up her dress.

She was not above shouting, "Hey, Pete, you missed a spot," or guffawing at the ludicrous inequities of life. In time, she offered me a drink.

But she refused to pay me for the day.

"You ain't done enough," she said. "When you're half done, you get fifteen more dollars. When you do the second coat, you get the rest."

"Frances," I said, "We agreed that I was working by the hour."

"You're nickel and diming me to death and you ain't halfway down one side. What do you think, I can't do math?"

"Frances," I said, mopping sweat from my brow, "I need a little."

"Have a drink, Pete," she said. "You look hot. You know you got my last six dollars."

Six bucks was enough if it had to be. Enough for a pint and some cigarettes.

I rinsed out my brush out and stashed it in a niche with the paint. "I don't know when I'll be back, Frances. We may have to renegotiate this deal."

"Pete, you bastard, I knew you were going to do this."

"One coat, Frances. Forget two coats. Get it out of your head."

"You get on down the road, then," she said. "Just git. If I had a dog, I'd sic him on you."

"One coat," I repeated, walking away. "One coat."

"You rascal. Next time you come around with your hand out, I'll box your ears. Don't think I won't."

She'd get over it. In a day or two, she'd need something else and she'd call for me like it never happened. No big deal.

There was no reason to mow Floyd's yard in the heat of the afternoon, so I sat in for a couple of numbers with The Make Do Band, and enjoyed the camaraderie that was developing between them as they combined their talents.

To find them still hard at it was a surprise. They had recorded a great deal of foolishness already that morning and had arrived at the conclusion that it was now time to get serious.

They were talking album covers when I came in.

"We could call it 'A Fool's Pair of Dice,'" said Floyd, "have a picture of Pete on the cover, with a funny hat, and dice in each hand. Up close, the dice can show snake eyes on every side."

"A funny hat?" I said, "Come on. What kind of hat?"

You know those surf hats with earmuffs that fold down. Like a hunting hat, but beachy, the wintry beachcomber look."

"How about a coonskin cap," suggested Walter.

"Davy Crocket, now." I said. "Is this is a comedy record."

"So far," said Floyd. "We must be the worst band in the world."

"That's it," said Walter. "Put that on the album cover in big letters. THE WORST BAND IN THE WORLD. That'll do it."

Two long handled paint brushes served my purpose as a drummer. A set of drum brushes and a snare drum would have offered a far wider set of possibilities, but I could make do with a typewriter case. A jazz drummer from way back, I was more than a match for any kind of curve they could throw.

"This song's real slow and simple," said Floyd, "I'm thinking a fifties highway wreck kind of sound, real solemn, with a drifty kind of melody and a talking vocal with an English accent, like Peter Noone, or Michael Caine, or that dwarf who played Mr. Wizard on t.v. Use your imagination when you hear my accent, you'll get the idea."

"Mr. Wizard?" Walter cocked an eyebrow at me.

"Forget him, think about this," said Floyd. "For the backup chorus, three Vietnamese girls singing, 'Johnny, oh, oh, Johnny,' all the way through. That'll be cool, yes?"

"Why three?" I asked.

"Ok, one. Imagine one. You think three's too many?"

"One's enough," I said. "More tender."

"Ok. One Vietnamese girl singing 'Oh, Johnny' in the background. We'll dub it in later. Meanwhile, if we're ready."

The living room was a maze of wires and microphones propped and draped and hung in place. Floyd had his finger poised on the pause button. Walter rattled the ice in his mug. "Hold it," he said, "hold everything. I need to fix another drink."

"Walter, please," said Floyd, "let's do this first. Man, we're right there. Let's cut this biscuit."

Walter set down his glass and counted us off. Floyd pushed the button and the Make Do Band recorded "Johnny Wrecked My Car." The rest, as they say on the hit parade, is history.

As I freshened up for my dinner engagement with Voris and Henry that evening, Floyd and Walter kept playing their newest recording over and over, amused to an absurd degree by humorous nuances audible only to the three of us.

"I like The Make Do Band," said Walter, "we need a better name, though."

"I was thinking the same thing," said Floyd.

"How about 'The Rubes'" I suggested..

"The Rubes." Walter laughed. "I like it."

"Meet The Rubes," said Floyd, "can you see that on the album cover?"

"The Rubes," Walter repeated. "Meet The Rubes."

Chapter Twelve
Dinner with the Goodnights,
or Can't Buy Me Love

The rewound tape began again. Walter watched me exit and said, "Hey, Pete, don't leave. Listen to this."

Floyd leaned his head out the door and called after me. "Don't worry about mowing the yard," he said, "just go on about your business. I'll hire some little neighbor boy."

At his use of the word 'hire,' I winced.

Floyd waved me on with a magnanimous gesture. His laughter had a wicked edge.

In his inimitable way he was warning me not to get comfortable in my little room. Any day I could be out on the street, depending on the force and temper of whatever winds did blow.

Walter's garage apartment remained vacant. If I could get in there, I could get some work done on the script. There was a whole section in the middle that needed a rewrite. Also, the chase scene was not what it could be. And there were letters to write, which required a certain amount of privacy. My gut ached for it every time I passed that empty bungalow.

Around the corner, the fumigation tent was gone from the Halloran house. An official notice posted on the front door threatened prosecution for trespassers. The windows were boarded up. I walked past the house and thought of the fortune hidden inside, unknown and unsuspected, hauntingly near yet so forbidden. Only in my imagination did I have the nerve to venture inside.

Flashlight in hand, navigating the attic rafters, bumping my head on low beams, tripping and falling into cushions of fiberglass insulation, I pictured myself maybe falling through the ceiling itself, breaking an ankle or hip bone, setting off a silent alarm, helpless to escape and being arrested, thrown in jail and charged with criminal trespass. Stunts involving cat burglary were not my forte'. But the money was there, in the piano and in various books. Someone undeserving was destined to find it and keep it. That, it seemed to me, was a worse crime than the one I contemplated.

A fraction of that money would have changed my circumstances in ways I dared not imagine. Most of it I would have given Arthur, for all I owed him over the years. When he was younger and still in college, Jenny worked and I was home writing my script. He'd loan me money for cigarettes and an occasional pint, as if he had it to lend, working a side job making sandwiches and going to school full-time. To my repeated promises to make it up to him when the script took off, he would say, "Don't worry about it." I can never repay him for the sacrifices he made for me. Even dropping a load of cash in his lap would be too little, too late. One thing I can do for him, I thought, as the pink house receded behind me, is keep myself out of jail.

Arthur wasn't the only one I owed. Numerous friends over the years had invested small amounts of cash in my script. A hundred here, two hundred there. I owed them all a final showing.

Voris' yard was a shaded wonderland, with tall ferns and rubber trees and a well-kept hedge that hung like a canopy over the patio. She was out in the yard, manicuring her well-tended garden. She had the portable telephone with her in a cumbersome shoulder pack.

She looked up and smiled when she heard me cough.

"Hi, Pete, come on in," she said, "I'm just puttering around out here. Henry's inside."

"You look vibrant today, Voris," I said, "rosy color in your cheeks. Very rosy."

"Don't make me blush," she said, "I'll embarrass myself."

Inside the door, Henry came toward me grinning, with his palm held out like I owed him money. I looked to Voris for an explanation.

"Give me five, Pete," he insisted.

When it dawned on me what he wanted I slapped his hand. He then slapped mine and added some arcane brother handshake and I went along with that, too. He seemed uncommonly glad to see me.

"Brother Pete," he said, "long time no see. What have you been doing with your bad self?"

"Well," I said, "I went to Tibet. Met the Dalai Lama. He sends his regards."

He laughed. "Wet the bed. That's funny. You ain't seen my computer room since I got it set up, have you?"

"No, but I have a feeling you're going to show me."

"Come on," he couldn't wait to drag me down the hall. "Wait till you see it, man. It's beautiful."

I looked back at Voris over my shoulder. She was smiling. "You two go on. I'll get dinner started."

"Irene, bring us a couple of beers, will you?" said Henry.

"Coming up," said Voris.

"Irene, that's cute," I said.

"Yeah, my little joke," said Henry. "Kind of funny. My first wife, I called her Irene, too. Her name was Ann. If I ever get married again—." He didn't finish the thought right away.

The computer room was designed to accommodate the entire spectrum of recreational software. Interrelated components covered one wall from the desk top to the ceiling. Various sized video screens enabled him to monitor several programs at once and record one or more on corresponding units. In a drawer of a filing cabinet was the videotape he had made of himself proceeding through the stages of assembly. He offered to play it for me sometime.

Voris brought our cold beers and left us alone. She kept her eyes lowered. A brief silence fell as she exited, dipping her chin to Henry in a servile bow, as a servant might curtsy, or a Catholic genuflect.

"All my wives name Irene," he said.

We sipped our beers. A feeling that it was going to be a long evening began to sink in.

Henry settled back in his swivel chair. There were no other chairs. When I leaned against the desk top, a semicircular plastic surface surrounding Henry on three sides, he said, "Don't sit there. Here, sit on this," and slid a little round hassock over to me, about a foot and a half tall. I lowered myself onto it and looked up at him, getting the full big me little you effect.

"What I really want to talk to you about is my new idea, Pete."

"Is it a big idea?"

"That's what I like about you, Pete. You're smart. You might not be as smart as you think you are, but you're smart enough to spot a good deal when you see one. So am I smart that way. That's why I know we can both make big money."

"With your big idea?"

"Yes!" He clenched his fist.

"I'm a captive audience," I said, stealing a glance at my watch.

"We can talk more about it later," he said. "Let's shoot some pool before you get a buttache from that hassock."

My knees were up around my armpits. Pool, badminton, any diversion would have been welcome. In the den I admired the factory showroom model, with its faux mahogany frieze ornately carved, and its polished chrome brightwork, grilled in an ostentatious diamond pattern.

"That's some table," I said, running my hand across the immaculate green felt.

Henry grinned, clicking two billiard balls together. "Feel like a game?"

"Sure," I said. "The object is what, to sink the eight ball, right?"

Henry started racking the balls. "There's a little more to it, but that's the idea. We'll play Detroit rules. Eight ball neutral."

"This is Florida," I said, "If you don't mind me asking, why are we playing Detroit rules?"

Henry shrugged. "That's the only way I know."

"Well, it's all the same to me," I said. "What does eight ball neutral mean?"

He frowned with disbelief. "Means you can combinate off the eight."

"I see," I said, "as opposed to not being able to uh, combinate off the eight, which I take it are the rules outside Detroit?"

"Right. You break."

"You can break," I said.

"I rack. You break."

"Is that a Detroit rule, too?"

"Just break, Pete. Bust them up."

I took aim down the long smooth stick and tried to remember the last time I had held one, or if I had ever held one. Maybe it was a smaller table, or maybe it was a movie I saw that merged with my subconscious. The table looked more vast than an airfield, the faraway pockets like hangars at the far end of the runway. I missed the cue ball several times, and learned that in the apt jargon of the game, my error was called a miscue. Voris mercifully called us in to dinner.

Henry hung his stick up, saying, "You surprise me, Pete. A worldly guy like you, I figured you must have played some pool. You didn't come up in no ghetto."

"Actually, I was very athletic as a young man. I played basketball and swam. Somehow pool never made it into my agenda. Of course, I regret that now. I think with a little practice I might have made a more respectable showing."

"You can come practice anytime, can't he, Henry?" said Voris

"Sure," said Henry. "We can talk some business."

"You set a lovely table, Voris."

"Thank you, Pete. Have some hush puppies."

"Don't mind if I do."

One thing was certain. I had not been eating properly for quite some time.

"Have you read any good books lately?" asked Voris.

I assumed she was asking me, but Henry answered her. "I read a good one," he said. "A true story. About a man who murdered his wife."

Voris shuddered. "Every book nowadays it seems is always about a murder. Your script isn't about a murder, is it, Pete?"

"As a matter of fact it is, Voris. Sorry to disappoint you. Several murders occur in the course of the story, but, though it takes the form of a murder mystery, I like to think of it as falling within the realm of comedy."

"I don't know what's so funny about murder, but I wish you all the luck in the world with it. I know you've been working at it God knows how long. Maybe your ship's about to come in, Pete. Wouldn't that be something? You with a hit movie and we could say we knew you when."

"That's very kind of you, Voris. The way things stand, I have no way of knowing how much longer it can take to get in the hands of the right people. I just need to hang in there. Keep plugging away."

Voris looked at Henry as if that were his cue.

"Pete," he said, "I've got an idea. I know you really want to make this movie, but meanwhile, you've got to make some green. Long green, you know what I'm saying?"

"Like I said before, I'm a captive audience."

Henry pushed his plate aside and Voris, catching a signal, began to clear the table. He took out a notepad covered with numbers and columns of figures.

"Wonderful dinner, Voris," I said.

"This is the deal," said Henry. "Dynamic Audio-Visual. That's the name of my company. I'm all set up on the computer nationwide with the wholesale prices on every kind of electronic equipment. I can get bargains you would not believe. That's where you come in." He leaned back and studied me, with his fingertips touching, poised below his chin. "I believe you're the right man for the job," he said, "but I could be wrong. Maybe you don't want to make a lot of money. Maybe you'd rather scuffle, and mow yards and paint for a living. You'll have to decide one way or the other what you want. I'm talking about a position here. Sales Manager." His hands went up as if to outline the title in the air between us. "I'm talking territory." He pulled out a map of the United States. The entire Southeastern sector was outlined in red. "All this can be yours, Pete." His eyes glittered with an eerie light, as if he were possessed by a demon, or, at the very least, a strain of megalomania. His hands went up in the air again. "Regional Sales Manager."

"Words fail me."

"Don't say anything now, Pete. Think about it for a couple of days. You can handle the advertising campaign I'm getting ready to mount. Pete, it's going to be big. We'll be rolling in bucks."

"That will be quite an experience."

"The thing is," he lowered his voice and drew closer, "I'm not sure how much longer we'll be staying in this location. We might be moving. If we do, we'll have to set you up some kind of way where we can maintain constant contact. How we'll manage that, I don't know, but don't worry, we'll figure it out. You just take some of this literature I've prepared for you home and look it over. These are wholesale price lists and suggested retail lists. Study it and tell me there ain't no money in this game."

"Thank you very much, indeed, Henry," I said. Stifling a yawn, I glanced at my watch. "Goodness, time does tick on. What a lovely dinner it's been, Voris, and a fascinating experience, as well, Henry. You've outlined quite an opportunity for someone with an aggressive and tenacious temperament. These are attributes I may not possess in sufficient quantities for your purposes. But then, how would I know? It's like pocket pool, right? You never know until you try."

"Right," Henry smiled. "You think about it."

"Bye, Pete," said Voris. "Thanks for coming by."

"My pleasure," I said. "Henry, Voris, Goodnight."

"Goodnight, Pete."

The door closed behind me and I shifted the weighty folder containing Henry's opportunity of a lifetime from one armpit to the other, thinking less about his grandiose idea than about what he had said about moving. Voris' house was paid for. Why would she move? Move where? Every possible scenario involved selling the house. Then what? Where would she be without her house?

In Henry's hands. In the benevolent care of her master.

That answer left me with an uneasy feeling.

Chapter Thirteen
An Elongated Concept of Time, or A Couple More Days

Floyd lay on the couch with his nose in lurid paperback. I glanced at the title: THEY EAT THEIR YOUNG.

"Another mystery?"

He looked up and nodded as I limped in. "Murder most foul."

There was a dull throbbing ache in my abdomen that was not unfamiliar. Sometimes, when I walked a great distance or otherwise strained myself my hernia would knot up. An egglike bulge would form below my beltline. With rest, the swelling usually went down by itself. The knot felt hard as a golf ball as I made my way to the stool by the kitchen counter.

"You all right?" Floyd asked.

"Fine," I said, ever mindful of the symptoms that had preceded my first hernia operation. Then, as now, I had felt weak. On that earlier occasion, Floyd had been quick to note my waxy yellow pallor. He and a friend, Lyle Stone, drove me straight to the Emergency Room and waited there for several hours with me until I was admitted.

My paperwork, that time, was already on file, which led to my case being expedited. Anticipating an unmanageable attack, I had begun the proceedings months in advance, providing the hospital with the requisite forms and waivers. Floyd would recall the form that required his notarized signature, stating that Peter Foster did indeed reside at his residence. "A mere formality," I had told him. "Without an official residence, they'll put me at the end of the line."

Floyd had signed it without enthusiasm. That notarized form was still on file, but had not been updated in over six months. That meant that in my records I had no official residence until Floyd signed and notarized an updated version of the residency affidavit. He never signed without protesting and calling it part of my "sandcrab" act.

"You don't look so good," said Floyd. "Hernia popping out again?"

"Afraid so," I said. "Maybe I just need to rest."

"If you're going to rupture, man, get in the car. Don't hesitate. If you need to go, let's go."

"I can't yet."

"Why not?"

"My paperwork needs to be updated," I said. "The residency statement."

"Another statement of residency," he said, in a bored voice that failed to mask his concern.

"You know what happens without it."

"We'll do it tomorrow," he said. "Then you go to the hospital. You're not dying here in this house."

"I'm not going to die."

"Not here, anyway," he said, "not if I can help it. Not living here, either."

"Your position's crystal clear on the subject," I said.

"Pete, I just don't see why it always has to be me. All the people you know and it's me you have to live with. Why can't you stay with Arthur? He can't put his own Dad up for a couple of months?"

My relationships with my sons were complicated. At any rate, they were not matters for discussion.

"Look, I like you, Pete, but I can't have you settling in here again. Last time, you stayed six months, remember? Asking you to leave didn't do any good. I had to shove you out the door. I had to rant and rave and you still put the guilt trip on me."

"Guilt trip?"

"Pete," he said, "when you go walking off down that road with your typewriter in one hand and your little red suitcase in the other, you look so pitiful, I can't begin to tell you. Like you missed your last bus. I can put you up for awhile, but six months is too long. So is five months. So is four months. So is three months. So is two months."

"How about one month?"

"That's the limit, Pete. That's all I can handle."

"Ok, kid," I said. "One month. I'll find something else by then. Say no more."

Floyd chuckled. "What it is, Pete," he said, "is that you have this elongated concept of time. You have a quasi Biblical notion of days where each day to you represents an arbitrary period; could be a month, or several million years. To God, too, it's just one day. That's how it is with you, too. You have a godlike overview of time, in general."

For a month, I could suffer his facetiousness in stride. As long as his wit amused himself, it served a purpose.

The next day, after a good night's rest, my hernia was much diminished. Floyd signed the statement of residency I had prepared, and Katie, in her first official act as a professional part-time notary public, notarized the form for a dollar.

She surprised us with the news that Walter was checking himself into detox. A man from the VA hospital had come to their house that morning and spoken with Walt. Walt got into the passenger seat of his car and rode off with the man without a word of protest.

Floyd and I sat on the porch and waved at Walter as he departed. "Guess that puts The Rubes on hold for awhile," I said.

"Guess so. Too bad, because Lyle wants to play with us." Floyd laughed. "He doesn't play any instruments, either, except the wooden xylophone. We could sure use a guitar player. Lyle can sing, but he always wants to ad-lib. Wally's the only guitar player I know, except for Arthur."

"Arthur's a bit more advanced," I said.

"Yeah, but who's he playing with? Nobody. He could have a lot of fun playing with us."

Floyd had no idea how out of his league Arthur was. Arthur's compositions were sophisticated and intellectual, very contemplative and classical.

"Primitive music is coming back," said Floyd. "Besides, we've got a variety of material. We could branch out into video comedy but first we need a good recording of some novelty songs, make it like borderline country, folk, comedy, reggae and/or rock. Run the gamut under the guise of misguided humor. If something clicks, maybe one song gets attention. Boom. We get them laughing, then we laugh last. It can be done."

"Sure it can," I said. Every man dreams a dream. "Arthur's very busy with his own compositions. Plus, he's been working long hours."

"Maybe he's just not Rube material," said Floyd.

Arthur's destiny was surely not to be a Rube. "You'll find another guitar player."

"I can't picture Walt sober," said Floyd. "Think he'll stay with it?"

"Detox may do him some good."

"For as long as it lasts."

"If he would just drink like a normal person."

"Like you?"

"You've never seen me drunk," I said. "Mellow, yes, not drunk."

"Walter can't get mellow. Once he dries out, it's going to be all or nothing for him."

"Keep looking for another guitar player," I said.

A couple of days turned into a couple of weeks. The days all ran together. Mr. Youngblood's house was finished a year to the day after I started it.

What Floyd had said about measuring time by my own standard was not without its kernel of truth. More and more it seemed like part of me was still living in the past. The dreams I had dreamed, the plans, the friends that were once an integral part of my life had grown nearer and dearer to me in their absence. A chorus of lost voices haunted my days as I walked through the heat of summer with a rake and a mower and pruning shears, taking little notice of the world around me, or of the time passing. My inner focus stayed fixed on a goal, which time could only deny me if I allowed my belief to waver.

Nights on a stool at the kitchen counter were spent typing letters into the early hours, keeping in touch with Rico in Vegas and with various contacts and friends in New York. In such matters, I kept scrupulous accounts of all my long distance calls. More often than not, the charges were reversed.

My second hernia operation went well, every bit the success of the first. Floyd was patient as I limped around for a couple of extra weeks over my deadline, knowing I had no money and nowhere to go. Then a check came from Rico, a hundred bucks, along with a note saying the worm was beginning to turn.

They kept Walt in detox for twenty-one days. He came home with a clear-eyed, healthy glow, a new man, so to speak. I offered him seventy-five bucks in cash and he let me move into the bungalow.

Chapter Fourteen
Home Away From Home,
or Return of the Stumbler

For once, moving was easy. Next door a vacant room awaited the tattered relics of my portable world. With the typewriter in place under the lamp on the desk I stepped back to savor the fine sensation of having a place of my own, a humble abode where I could smoke at will and collect my thoughts at my own leisure. Walter sat on his front steps drinking a big glass of lemonade and watching me pass back and forth from Floyd's with boxes and bags containing my meager possessions.

"What have I done?" he implored the heavens, "What have I done?"

What indeed? Aside from violating the terms of his lease, and jeopardizing the purchase of the house, what had he done? His good faith and generosity were sure to be rewarded. In preventing an independent film producer such as myself from being mistaken for a common vagrant, he was investing in the future of film, and in his own future as well, for he now had in his possession an affidavit with my signature entitling him to a one percent share of any and all net profits I might yet derive from the sale or production of my screenplay, including any related merchandising revenues such as T-shirts, coloring books, hats, or sunglasses. The value of that document could not be estimated. As for placing in peril his newfound state of sobriety, Katie had already cautioned me not to drink in front of him.

Her little warning, of course, presaged his doom.

I had no intention of influencing Walter. The very fact that I was there in my apartment every night, typing, while in the room adjacent Walter underwent his lonely struggle, was reason enough to link me with his relapse. The blame might as easily be Katie's, for failing to stave off his onslaughts of loneliness by sacrificing her last two bingo nights. Her steep reduction from seven bingo nights a week to two was a voluntary withdrawal that carried its own peculiar brand of strain.

Ever hopeful, Katie accepted his recovery as a fait acompli, yet was unable to believe that outside influences such as myself posed no threat to that recovery. As I tried to explain to her several times, his newfound resolve to forswear the imbibition of spirits would come with a diabolical talent for rationalization. His nemesis would be, not me, but the proverbial devil on his shoulder.

The initial two weeks went well. Walter drank lemonade and tea by the gallon. He was rehired at the station on a probationary basis. His guitar playing improved dramatically, his rhythms sounding crisper, sharper, more defined. In two Rube sessions on tape the evidence was audible. Still, the notion was lodged in his mind that his most creative moments were either fueled or inspired by alcohol. In one breath, he denounced his addiction, in the next, he romanticized it as the wellspring of all rarefied inspiration. On the surface, he appeared calm and unhurried, neither impressed nor unimpressed with sobriety.

Far too often, he would seek me out, wanting to talk. He would come through the adjoining door to my room, which had no lock, without knocking, and approach my desk where revisions of a critical ten page section of my script preoccupied my attention.

Once he came in and I happened to have page ninety-nine in the typewriter, having just crumpled up that same page and tossed it into a wastebasket overflowing with discarded versions of that troublesome page. A fresh sheet was scrolled in and numbered, as was my habit, and I was resting my tired eyes. Glasses removed, forehead resting on the backs of my forearms, crossed on top of the typewriter carriage, I often slept in that position. If my eyes were watery, it had nothing to do with the script. I may have been thinking of Arthur, and perhaps a sob of sorts did escape from my heart in a moment I had every reason to believe was private and unobserved. Precisely then, Walter placed his hand on my shoulder and asked, "What's wrong, Pete? Why are you crying?"

"Just resting my eyes, Walt," I said.

"What's the matter, Pete?" he persisted. "Page ninety-nine got you down?"

The notion that page ninety-nine or any page could cause me a single melancholy moment was ludicrous. The moment was over almost before it began.

Walter wanted to talk, not so much about my script, though that subject, once it came up, was covered. He preferred to talk about his favorite subject, alcohol. Did I have any?

"No," I lied. "And if I did, what kind of friend would I be if I told you about it?"

"Oh, I don't want any," he said, "I just wondered if any was around. If it was close by, and I still didn't want any, I figure I'd know then that I was all right."

"Walter," I sighed. "Walter, Walter, Walter." The transparence of his subterfuge cast a pall over his commitment to teetotalism.

"Katie can't know if I do have a drink," he said in a conspiratorial undertone, as if we were henchmen of sorts involved in a covert subplot. "Katie needs to be kept completely in the dark if I ever do drink. Because she'd leave me. She would."

"You're very lucky to have her, Walter."

"That's why she can't find out," he said.

"Walter, are you tipping a little in secret?"

"No," he said, "not yet, but if I do, if, I ever do have one drink, I know what'll happen. I'll be driving along maybe listening to the radio and the car will drive itself to the liquor store. I won't be able to stop myself. I'll buy a bottle and that'll be that. If that happens, I'm going to need for Katie not to know about it for as long as possible. She might not leave me, but she might, you know, if she thinks I started drinking again. Which I haven't. I don't even want a drink. But if you want one, Pete, go ahead. You can drink in front of me."

Courtesy dictated the only acceptable response to that suggestion. Ignoring it, I went to the sink and poured a glass of tap water.

"Pete," he said, "I'm not holding you up, am I? You want me to leave? You want to get back to your script, don't you? How's it coming? Still on page ninety-nine? That must be a hell of a page."

"Yes, Walter," I said, "a hell of a page."

"Well, you get back to it," he said, without moving. "I'm not bothering you, am I?"

"Well, to be frank with you, Walter," I said. "I would like to get a little work done tonight if that's possible."

"I understand," he said. "You want to watch some television?"

"No, Walter, thanks, but I'm on a roll here. I'll put in a few more hours before I turn in."

"Want some lemonade, Pete? I've got great lemonade. Real tasty."

"No, thank you, Walter."

"Tea?"

"No. A glass of coke, maybe, if you have any."

"We're out of coke. I have tea and lemonade, Pete. Tea and lemonade."

"Pass," I said.

"That's what I said in my dream last night."

"You dreamed of lemonade?"

"No, I dreamed about booze. Ever dream about booze, Pete?"

"Not so much, no."

"Try dreaming about booze sometime, then wake up and have yourself a big glass of lemonade."

"Walter," I said, "if you're going to drink, please don't involve me. I've got a movie to make here and I don't have time to sit around and debate the issue. Caminiti's been in touch with a guy named

Jerry, Jerry Pannatore. He can bankroll this film by himself if he wants to. Pull five mil out of the wall safe and lay it on the line. He's done it before and made money"

"Is he going to make your movie?"

"This Jerry guy's very low key. But he's got bread. And he's got the script. It may be sitting on his desk right now under a pile of other scripts, but he's got it. Rico's given him the pitch. So these revisions are very important. They have to be done and in the mail to Rico so that he has them in hand the next time he talks with Jerry. If Jerry has any questions or doubts at that point, these ten pages could very well be the deciding factor."

"I hope you do make this movie, Pete," said Walter. "You're intelligent. You're a writer, an actor, a painter, a drummer, a yard man. You're good at everything you do."

"Thank you, Walter."

"But you know what else you are?"

"No, Walter, what else am I?"

"You're a drunk."

"I am not a drunk, Walter."

"Deny it all you want. That's called 'denial.'"

"I know what it's called. Walter, if I take a drink, it doesn't make me a drunk. Lots of people drink. It doesn't mean they're all drunks."

"But you are. Ask anybody."

"Walter, I am perfectly fine. My mind is clear. My hands are steady. I've never even had a hangover."

"I'm an alcoholic, Pete. There's no doubt in my mind. I'm one of the obvious ones. You're a little different."

"Thank you, Walter, for that vote of confidence."

"Don't get pissed off, ok, Pete? The other day, I counted the empty pint bottles of Dark Eyes you've been collecting under the house. Nineteen dead soldiers, Pete. Under just one corner. You've got them piled under every corner."

"They're not mine," I said.

"No one else drinks that cheap vodka, Pete."

"Walter, I have work to do."

"You want me to leave?"

"If you don't mind."

"Ok, Pete," he said. "You sure you don't want to watch some television?"

"Not tonight."

"All right. See you tomorrow."

I lit a cigarette as he left the room and pushed my chair back. Page ninety-nine had waited this long, it could wait a little longer. Any flow I had was gone.

Outside in the cool night air I stared up at the stars in the bright September sky. Jenny's birthday was coming up on the tenth.

Half buried in the ground, I had a pint hidden under a pile of broken bricks. Walter had no qualms about going through my things. In that little room, he'd have found a bottle. What he had said about me being a drunk was unworthy of comment, coming from him. I poured a little vodka in my water glass and sipped it sparingly, remembering other times and Jenny, making the same charge against me.

After Peter died, Jenny's mother came to stay. Someone had to look after Hilary. No nursing home was worthy. Jenny's byline appeared in print each day. In contrast with my belabored output, it was evident whose writing career was vital, and whose had stalled. We laughed together about it then, but the decision to move to Shadville Beach had been hers, not mine. When Jenny sent her resumes out, she covered all the bases. We moved here when she got the job and we stayed because she kept her job at the *Clarion-Tribune*.

From the beginning, it just wasn't my town. Jobs came and went, but my work was writing. The screenplay I had high hopes for made the rounds and was finally put away. I began another one and for years it grew without maturing. I drank in moderation while the boys grew and life went on.

To my knowledge, there was no single point when my sons lost respect for me. Long before Jenny divorced me, I had become someone I never expected to be. A drunken failure, Jenny said.

Bradley said the same. Arthur, if he ever thought it so, never put it to me in so many words. He understood that I was made of sterner stuff, and not to be counted out.

Bradley made no bones about it. He was ashamed of me. Arthur had the grace to be torn, at least, between conflicting emotions.

A few days earlier, I'd been to see Arthur at his apartment. Bradley made his usual brief appearance, changed his clothes and left, with a 'Hi, Dad' and a 'Bye, Dad.' Arthur surprised me with a video copy of *The Brain That Wouldn't Die*. We watched it together again that evening, replaying my scene in the film over and over.

"I'm keeping this tape, Dad," he said. "The video store will charge me twenty bucks or so for losing it, but don't worry. I'll have it. Also, I did a little sleuthing through the database at the video store and located *The Brides Wore Blood*. There's like one copy in the whole state, at a motel on the west side of town that rents horror flicks and porno to the guests."

"Who rents horror movies at a motel?"

"All kinds, Dad. You're big in the pillow trade. The desk clerk said he can't rent it unless you rent a room, but he'll sell it outright for twenty-eight bucks."

"Arthur, that may be the only copy in the whole world."

"If it is," he said, "you'll have to get it. I can't afford to buy both of them."

"I'll get it."

He gave me the address of the motel and I started studying bus routes and schedules. To get to the westside location meant changing buses three or four times. As for the twenty-eight bucks, I'd figure some way to get around paying it all at once. Somehow, we'd get it and watch it together. Arthur was only about nine when that movie was made.

No obscure horror film was more obscure than *The Brides Wore Blood*.

The doorbell rang, jarring me out of my reverie with a most melodious ring.

Arthur was in the shower, so I answered the door. An attractive woman, smartly dressed, with reddish blonde hair and no glasses stood holding an overnight bag.

"I brought these for Arthur," she said, and her voice gave me a start. "Hello, Peter," she said.

"Hello, Jenny."

Only her voice gave her away. Stunned at the tricks of the mind and eye that allowed me not to recognize the woman who was my wife, I stood in the doorway and stared at her. She looked ten years younger with contact lenses and a new hairdo. But that look in her eyes was as cold as the north wind. She still longed to crush me.

"I can't stay," she said.

"No, please," I said, stepping aside to let her in. "Arthur's just in the shower. I'm on my way out. You're looking well, Jen."

"You should take better care of yourself, Peter."

Had she not taken me off her insurance I might have had my teeth fixed, at least. Nodding in pointless agreement, I closed the door behind me, amazed that I could look at Jenny and see a stranger.

Walter's screen door squeaked open and banged shut as I tucked the bottle back under a brick. A second or two passed before Walter approached in the moonlight.

"Hey, Pete," he said. "Katie's not back from bingo yet. What you drinking there, bud?"

I drained the glass. "Just water."

"Got any more of that good bottled water?"

"Walter, are you going to keep bugging me for a drink every time I see you? I promised Katie."

"I promised her too," he said. "Let's have a little drink, Pete."

"No."

He looked around in the moonlit rubble near my feet. "What's that right there under that rock?"

"Ok, Walter," I said. "You want a drink? Here, have a drink." I handed him the pint, which had about two fingers left in it. He looked at the bottle just long enough to decide it was no use resisting. Then he unscrewed the cap and tilted back a little shot. He handed it back to me. I felt disgusted, but I killed the rest before he had a chance to, and tossed the empty under the house with the others.

"Katie can't know," he said.

"Of course not."

The sound of a cat screeching split the night. Over Walter's back fence, in the Halloran yard, two toms were hissing and clawing in a brief but intense flurry. In the silence that followed, we looked at the pink house glowing under the full moon.

"You know," Walter said, "there's supposed to be money in that house. Lester told me."

"Did he say where it is?"

Walter shook his head. "I couldn't find it."

"You were in there? When?"

"Only once. The place stinks ungodly."

"When were you in there?"

"A couple of nights ago. You need a gas mask in there."

"Where did you look?"

"Just around. I was scared of getting caught in there. They'd put me away for that."

Something kept me from telling him the money was in the piano. Maybe it was Katie's car pulling into the drive just then. Walter popped a stick of gum in his mouth and walked over to greet her. Page ninety-nine was waiting for me inside, but all I could think about was the money in the Halloran piano.

Chapter Fifteen
Bit Part Player, or The Ghoul

The haunting image of a baby grand staked a residency claim in my imagination, its fine mahogany grain obscured beneath a layered encrustation of dust and decades old grime, its innards hoarding a secreted fortune in large denominational bills, stuffed at random through the wires, scattered in absent minded haste in uncounted piles no accountant alive deserved to see. The vision rooted in the back of my mind, invading my dreams and weighing down my days with an insidious yearning to commit a harmless and victimless crime.

Though I lacked the derring-do to disregard the criminality of my fantasized misdeed and pursue the base urge come what may, I was neither able nor willing to dismiss the opportunistic scheme out of hand. The idea was far too intriguing to abandon for righteousness' sake.

Not that I felt righteous. In a moral sense, I was already guilty of coveting my neighbor's goods, and subject to the metaphysical consequences of breaking that minor commandment. In my view, I might yet be spared the penalty for coveting if I adhered to the virtuous principles of good citizenship and maintained a philosophical outlook.

Call it cowardice, or discretion, it was the better part of a foolhardy conscience that kept me away from the pink house.

Like the dog protecting the manger from the ox, I found myself in the perversely proprietary position of preserving the piano's mythic integrity from aimless night stalkers such as Walter, whose moral laxity stood in stark contrast to my own considered code of conduct.

Day by day, I weighed the notion of taking him into my confidence and letting events then run their course. Never one to act on impulse, I pondered every aspect of my dilemma without making a firm decision.

With my new bus schedule brochures, and all my changes and times routed, I set out early one morning on the B bus, got off downtown at Forsyth and Pearl, walked three blocks to Adams and caught the N bus to the Normandy Boulevard mall. The H bus took me from there to Westchester Heights, where, on the fringes of the fabled Orange Blossom Trail, near the rusted railroad tracks a block from the exit to 295, stood a little mom and pop motel called the Gator Lodge.

The Gator Lodge was undistinguished in the extreme. Apart from the office building, which was new, nothing on the exterior set the establishment apart from the thousands of one story brick motels that once sprinkled the length and breadth of Florida. Built in the bungalow style of the fifties, each unit was a separate small house, twelve or fourteen units in all. Same beds, same seascapes and fishing scenes on the walls. Instead of quarter slot bed vibrators, the rooms offered a range of video privileges to the guests.

A discreet catalog was available upon request at the front desk, listing hundreds of available titles in America's two most popular genres, horror and sex.

In my tentative plan of action, devised during the bus ride over, I would engage the desk clerk in superfluous conversation, improvising mannerisms to put him at ease, ask to see a catalog, peruse it, and react with sophisticated amusement at the presence in it of the title, *The Brides Wore Blood*. From there I would wing it and persuade him somehow to allow me the privilege of borrowing the tape for twenty-four hours in order to make a copy.

An optimistic plan. The desk clerk was the variable. Once I made my entrance, I would have to clue into some facet of his character without delay. The distance from the door to the front desk was less than ten feet. If I walked slowly, accenting the age and the sympathy bit, I could gain about a minute, time enough to peg the clerk into some sort of category. Then it would be showtime.

I pushed open the smoked glass door to the lobby, half-expecting to find a cretinous redneck behind the desk with a shotgun hanging on the wall beside his Klan photos. Instead, a paraplegic man in an electric wheelchair looked up with intelligent eyes from his book, a scientific tome, and asked how he might be of assistance.

James Mason's distinguished manner came to mind as I cleared my throat of a pesky tickle and without further ado I became a peer of the realm.

"How do you do, sir?" I said. "My name is Fenway, Philip Fenway. I'm a collector of cinematic oddities. If you would be so kind, may I peruse your catalog of videotapes?"

"Be my guest," said the young man, directing his chair toward me with a quiet electronic hum. He placed a dogeared stack of stapled typescript pages on the counter and retreated. "What sort of cinematic oddities do you collect?" he asked.

"Primarily horror," I said. "Low budget obscurities. There's a cultish fascination abroad for certain titles. Curious phenomena, that. By the way, you handle that wheelchair with admirable dexterity, if you don't mind my saying so."

The young man studied me, no doubt struck by the anomaly of my frayed shirt collar, which bespoke a less well fixed identity than I meant to convey as I thumbed through the catalog, scanning at my leisure, raising an occasional eyebrow at the lewdness of a title.

"My son, Bradley," I volunteered, after a moment, "was afflicted with polio as a child. By the grace of God, he recovered. He was the poster child for the *March of Dimes* in 1972."

"He was very lucky. You both were," he said. "I have muscular dystrophy."

There it was, the thread that linked us. "You do very well, son,"

I said. "Pardon me, I don't mean to call you son. In those days, I was very close to my son and now that he is healthy as a horse, I seldom see him anymore."

"My father is dead," he said.

"Mother, too?"

"She lives in Tampa with my sister."

"You're not alone, then."

"I'm not complaining."

"Of course not. May I ask your name?"

"Michael," said the young man, rolling forward again to extend his hand in friendship. We shook hands.

"A pleasure to meet you, Michael."

He smiled. "Nice to meet you, Mr. Fenway. Will you be wanting a room?"

"No, I have some friends at the beach," I said. "House-sitting for them while they're away." My heart leaped at the sight of *The Brides Wore Blood* notation in the catalog. "Michael, if I may speak frankly, I'd like to tell you why I'm here."

"You don't want a room?"

"Correct." The catalog was open to the page listing and I turned it toward him with my finger on the notation. "In 1973," I said, "when my son, Bradley, was still on crutches, I was involved in the production of several low-budget films, many of which were lost in a mysterious fire. One in particular was *The Brides Wore Blood*, a rarity which survived the fire but was also for lack of a better word, lost, when the director and producer, Mr. Lee Jennings, died leaving his affairs in disarray. Mr. Jennings' widow claimed no knowledge of its whereabouts, and for years my inquiries drew a blank. Then, after extensive research on his employer's computer, my other son, Arthur, who works in a video store part-time, located a video tape here, in your catalog, after all these years. A very intriguing question, to my mind, is how it came to be here? Who's handling it?"

"All these films come out of Philly," he said.

"Probably a syndicate of some sort. You do have a copy, then? May I see it?"

"Unless it's checked out." He consulted a computerized filing system. "There's just the one copy. Not a big item here."

"Or anywhere," I said.

"Kind of a weird flick," said Michael. "Here it is." He handed me the videotape, the grail, *The Brides Wore Blood*. A lascivious drawing on the cover depicted a seductive blonde impaling her womb with a large hunting knife and blood spilling down her white wedding gown. The picture gave an inaccurate view of the scene in the film, in which she used a shard of glass, not a knife, but that was beside the point. My hands cupped it like an artifact.

"You were involved in the production?" said Michael, with interest. "What did you do?"

"I was the ghoul," I said. "They conjured me from a pentagram."

"That was you?"

"Indeed, yes," I said. "Michael. I must have a copy of this tape."

"You can have that one for twenty-five bucks."

"Michael, I don't have twenty-five dollars. But my son, Arthur, can duplicate this copy at the store. I can have it back to you no later than tomorrow."

"Sorry, Mr. Fenway, I can't release it."

"You have my word as a gentleman."

"Without a cash deposit, my hands are tied. I have to account for all these tapes."

"What kind of cash deposit?"

"Ten bucks."

"I'll bring you the ten when I return the tape tomorrow."

He found that amusing. "Is that really you, the ghoul, in that swordfight?"

"Are you kidding? That was a real sword! I thought it was rubber. He slashed at me for eight minutes with a machete. He cut me with it, right below the eye. When we finished that scene, I went to Lee and said, 'Hey, I'm bleeding here,' But yes, to answer your question, yes. None other. Michael, Mike, have a heart. My sons have never seen this movie. For them, please, not for myself, I'm asking for twenty-four hours."

Film buffs are all the same. The dream of magic reaches places in their hearts no words can touch. Michael was thinking he'd never see me or the tape again. He was right.

"You make it hard to say no to you, Mr. Fenway."

"I'll take good care of it, Michael."

"Do you have some identification."

"Not a scrap."

"Driver's license, anything."

"My license expired. I no longer drive."

"How do you cash your checks?"

"What checks?"

He shook his head and studied me. "Is anything you said true?"

"Every word, except my name. Peter Foster," I said, extending a hand across the desk. "I can't tell you what this means to me, Michael."

He couldn't help smiling as we shook hands. "You're a piece of work, mister."

"As are you, sir."

He turned his eyes to the ceiling and began to whistle. I was out the door.

On the bus, with the grail under my shirt next to my heart, I hummed the theme to *The Man From La Mancha*.

I could hardly wait to see Arthur. But I headed for home to freshen up first. Floyd was in the front yard on a dropcloth again, with another piece of furniture, rubbing a coat of tung oil into the mahogany grain of an oblong block of wood. The brass foot pedals belonged to a baby grand piano.

A woman who was considering having her piano refinished wanted a sample so she could see what kind of finish to expect before he started. "I've never done a piano before," he said, as he turned the piece slowly in the air against the evening sunlight. "Kind of has to be perfect."

His enthusiasm exceeded the realm of craftsmanship. The

image of a baby grand piano gleamed behind his eyes. More than a love of fine wood, more than a table or a chest of drawers would inspire, something about a piano inspired a spark of lust.

He carried the piece inside when Lyle Stone arrived with his date, the lovely Jane. The three of them were going out somewhere. I showed them the tape I had acquired and explained some of its modest history to them. Their response warmed my heart. Jane made a fuss over me. She wanted to take us all back to her house right away to watch it on her VCR.

Arthur and I were going to screen it that night, I told them. After he made a copy, we could all get together sometime and watch both movies.

"That would be so great," said Jane. "We'll have a film festival. The Peter Foster Film Festival!"

You know you've arrived when they name a festival after you.

By the time I got to Arthur's it was dark. As I was appreciating the clavichordian nuances of the ring, he opened the door part way and said, "Well?"

I gave him the barest perceptible nod. He opened the door to let me in and closed it behind me. I tossed the tape on top of the VCR and said, "Plug it in, son, my conscience is bothering me. I had to shuck and jive a little crippled boy to get it."

"This better be good, Dad."

"Arthur," I said, "you don't know how long I've been looking forward to this."

"Roll 'em," said Arthur, as the screen began to flicker. He turned down the lights. Then the letters across a field of blue read: Regal King Features, Inc.

"Who in the hell are they?" I wondered.

Then the movie started, and I watched it with my son. I was the most fortunate of men.

Chapter Sixteen
The Peter Foster Film Festival or,
The Actor That Wouldn't Die

Due to the grainy quality of the original, the copy Arthur made had color problems. For twenty-four hours that bothered me, then I allowed that I had done my best to keep my promise to Michael and que sera sera.

Watching that film with Arthur took me back to the days of its production and I found myself remembering scenes and conversations behind scenes and where I stood during certain scenes and how they were shaped from the formless structure of Lee's original script. He didn't even have a shooting script after the second day. He was shooting the architecture of Flagler College and asking me what I thought about the movie so far.

"Movie?" I said, "what movie?" All I'd seen was a lot of people standing around. Nobody knew the story. "You've got a vampire, Lee. What else? What happens in the script?"

"The script is shit," he said. "Let's do something different."

"Fine," I said, "what?"

"Whatever comes to mind," he said.

"Let's take another look at the script," I said. "There must be something worth saving."

In scene after scene I recognized the restraining influence of a nameless script consultant. Lee Jennings had an alarming tendency to branch out in fifty different directions, scattering red herrings hither and yon and following no single thread to its conclusion. His was not an organized mind.

Arthur appreciated the bold amalgam of derivative plotlines and the underlying element of satire, a facet of the film Lee never recognized. Lee insisted the film was serious, even while he laughed as much as anybody at the absurdity of the premise and some of the scenes. And when I recommended he target the college fraternities, who were famous for turning obscurities into bona fide cult classics, like *Killer Clowns From Outer Space*, for instance, or *Attack of the Killer Tomatoes*, Lee went vague and mentioned mysterious other plans for distribution.

At the time videotapes were unheard of, so any deal made with Regal King Features, Inc. came much later, and had to involve someone other than Lee, who was dead a month after the opening, which was held at the Pinetop Theater in Fernandina Beach on a Sunday afternoon.

The debut was supposed to headline a triple feature horror show, but the ad copy went to the newspapers with a significant error intact and the result was that *The Brides Wore Blood* made its grand debut to an audience of surfers who had gathered to watch *The Endless Summer* and *Ride the Wild Surf*.

Needless to say, it was not a big hit. Lee was desolated. The theatre was empty before the opening credits were through rolling. We sat and watched it, he and I, along with some of the cast and crew who stayed.

"It's terrible," he said.

"Nothing's perfect, Lee," I said. "God knows, it could have been worse."

"What if we gave it subtitles? Dubbed it in Spanish, you know Spanish, don't you, Pete?"

"What would you do with it then?"

"Hell," he said. "Show it in Miami. I'm thirty grand into this dog. I need to get out from under."

Less than a month later his studio was destroyed by fire. Lee was trapped inside, along with, according to Mrs. Jennings, all the copies of *The Brides Wore Blood*.

"That darn arithmetic," said Arthur.

"At any rate," I said, "there it is. My farewell to film."

Arthur laughed, "Want to watch it again, Dad?"

We watched it two more times that night.

In the early hours, as I was leaving, Bradley came home with a girl named Taffy. Arthur had just gone to bed. I offered a brief encapsulation of the history of the film for them as it rewound. The pair settled into the deep cushioned couch with the lights turned low and a bag of chips on the coffee table. I pushed play and watched until my name rolled by on the opening credits. In deference to romance, I made a quiet exit.

"Goodnight, Dad," said Bradley.

"Goodnight, Mr. Foster," said Taffy.

The film festival proper was organized by Jane and scheduled for a Saturday afternoon two weeks hence. My celebrity stature increased exponentially with each passing day. Overnight, I had become a personage of note in the neighborhood, and through my comportment reflected an unwavering modesty, the respectful, even deferential regard to my friends for my person was nonetheless gratifying. But no, I assured Floyd, I was not one to forget the little people who had known me in humbler days.

Floyd was most concerned that I, as guest of honor, be sartorially correct. He had a white silk dress shirt in his closet with European lines, which couldn't have fit me better if it were tailored. Of course, I had no cufflinks, but he insisted I wear it.

"You look like a hipster, Pete," he said. "Here, try this on. Try this." He started pulling clothes out of his old clothes closet, a pair of motheaten dress pants; not quite my size, and an old tweed jacket with wide lapels that Chico Marx or some immigrant gypsy boy might have worn to Ellis Island in the Thirties.

"I'll pass on the jacket," I said.

"What? You don't like it?" I couldn't tell if he was serious or not.

"You wear it," I said.

He hung it back up. "I keep it around for Halloween," he said. "You never know."

"The shirt's fine," I said. "I'll just roll up these sleeves."

"No, I got some cufflinks for you. Wait, where are they?" He went into his room and came back with a pair of Alfred E. Neuman cufflinks, featuring the gold-plated visage of the MAD magazine icon above his immortal motto, WHAT ME WORRY?

"What a kidder," I said.

"No, really, just wear them," he said. "They're a collector's item."

He took my wrists one at a time and inserted them in the cuffs. "OK, my man," I said. "What next? A string tie?"

"Too Texas," he said, after a moment's thought, "can't have you looking like some foppish ne'er do well. Besides, I don't have one. You need shades. Here." He handed me sunglasses. "I wish I had a cool derby hat for you, with a snap brim like Bat Masterson."

"No hat," I said, patting my sparse but well groomed hair. I put the sunglasses on. "What am I, a cowboy?"

He shrugged, "A big Harley Davidson belt buckle would look sharp."

"Not without a string tie," I said.

"You don't have any boots, do you? Never mind. Sneakers will do. Keep the shades on when you make your entrance. Trust me. You look like Bix Beiderbecke."

"What is *Young Man With a Horn?*" I said instantly. I could have made a fortune on *Jeopardy*.

Without my real glasses, I had difficulty seeing through the shades, but I managed to follow Floyd outside and into his van. In my gentleman's attire I felt like a distinguished blind man, minus the cane, as I made an effort to focus through the dark glasses on the blurring neighborhood. My sight was fading. I composed my features into a mask of impassive dignity, and waited with the two precious videotapes in hand, for a sign from Floyd that we were there.

"Don't let me trip on the red carpet," I said.

There was a hand-lettered sign on a poster board tacked above the lintel at Jane's house and crepe streamers festooned the screened porch in front. Without my glasses, I had to be told that it said THE PETER FOSTER FILM FESTIVAL.

Jane and Lyle came out to greet me. Jane's friend, Carol, and her two daughters began clapping as Lyle handed me a cold beer and let me into the house. The girls, no older than ten or twelve appraised me quickly, clapping as instructed. They soon returned to their outdoor play, which involved chasing one another and throwing sandspurs at each other's long hair.

I was led to the seat of honor, a deep leather recliner positioned in front of the television, and introduced formally as the man of the hour. Most of the guests I knew, Floyd and Lyle and Jane, of course. I met Carol, mother of Mimi and Samantha, her boyfriend, Huckie, who had a prosthetic leg, and Annette, another friend of Jane's, who taught music at the same inner city high school where Jane taught Spanish.

Annette was an attractive woman of African descent. As she shook my hand, her smile was refreshing. "A pleasure to meet you," she said. "I understand you're also a writer and a musician."

"A drummer," I said, "I used to play a little jazz."

"I love jazz," she said.

Carol was next in the queue. She was a tall blonde with cool blue eyes that looked familiar. "Didn't you mow my lawn one time?" she asked. "These are my daughters, Mimi and Sam, Samantha."

The two girls smiled and curtsied, then hurried off again. They both had appalling overbites from habitual thumbsucking.

From time to time, the floating sounds of their mischievous banter or a scrap of childish dialog would permeate the din of adult conversation in the room, such as when Mimi, the younger girl, with pathetic bravado boasted to her sister, "I have drank bleach before."

An old instinct, ever alert to alarming nuances in the voices of children, seized on the mental picture of an unfortunate child drinking bleach. At the same time, I was aware that their mother remained nonplussed, content to leave the girls to their own devices.

Huckie was last in the welcome line. "Hi, Pete," he said. "I'd have a beer with you, but I'm not supposed to drink."

"Hell, have a beer," said Lyle, "it's a party."

"Maybe one," said Huck. "Since Carol's been going to Al-Anon with Jane, she's been giving me hell about drinking. Hell, she drinks. You wait. It won't be me who starts a ruckus, I guarantee."

"Huckie!" Carol's voice carried a threat.

He held up one finger to signify to her that it was his first and, so far, only beer.

Jane came forward then, announcing that she, for one, couldn't wait any longer. There was food on the kitchen table and paper plates in readiness, a cooler full of beer and cold drinks, wine and vodka in the kitchen. She picked up the tapes and inspected them, cringing at the bloody artwork.

She asked which one to play first.

"The other one," I said. "*The Brain That Wouldn't Die*. Definitely,"

As the screen began to flicker the room fell silent. All eyes observed the opening credits, alert for appearance of my name.

"I'm only a walk on in this one."

"To us, you're a star," said Jane. "You're the only movie star we know."

"The beginning's kind of slow, isn't it?" said Floyd.

"The reason for that," I explained, "is that there were two different directors and two different scripts. They tried to patch it together and that never works."

"Can we fast forward it to your part?" asked Floyd.

"No, we will not!" Jane was shocked at the suggestion. "We will watch the entire movie."

"And a darn good one it is," said Floyd.

"Leave him alone, Floyd," said Lyle, gruffly. "Pete, you ready for a drink?"

"Don't mind if I do," I said, beginning to get up.

"Don't get up," said Lyle. "How do you want it?"

I was already up and moving toward the kitchen.

"Show me how you want it and I'll bring your next one," said Lyle. "I'll be your personal bartender."

"My own bartender," I said. "I have arrived."

"Ok, this much ice, this much vodka, this much coke, right?"

"Fine."

"This is a weird drink, Pete."

"Weird?"

"Vodka and coke?"

"Suits me, barkeep."

"Hey, Pete," said Lyle, "Floyd Tarlton's an asshole to make fun of your movie."

"He's just trying to be funny."

"At your expense. This movie must mean a lot to you."

"Not that much," I said.

"Then you don't mind if I laugh at it, too?"

"Be my guest."

Behind his drooping mustache, a grin widened. "You're alright, Pete," he said, clapping me on the back. "You ain't much but you're alright."

Lyle Stone was perhaps a bit mystified by the durability of my friendship with Floyd. In his solicitous concern for my feelings, I detected a probe. He may have been astounded by the heroic patience with which I endured Floyd's condescension.

Nothing could be simpler to explain. Floyd knew me. When I was hard up, he'd take me in. Around Christmas, he was always good for at least two weeks.

More than that, we went back fifteen years. We met on a painting job when Floyd was a college student, working part time. He had a yen to write and we became friends because I was a writer. I supposed that was the main reason. He couldn't have known many writers in Shadville Beach.

Over the years, our paths kept crossing. Years passed in the intervals, but he would appear and reappear and I would bring him up to date on the events in my life.

When Peter died, I walked around in a daze. I hadn't seen Floyd for several years. One day a cab pulled up beside me. Floyd was driving. He opened the door. "Hey kid," I said. It was like I'd just seen him the day before yesterday. I told him about Peter and he dropped me off at home.

The sporadic hostility between Lyle and Floyd was much more a matter of rivalry. Ill-concealed resentment, exacerbated by Lyle's ungoverned jealousy over Jane's platonic friendship with Floyd came into play. A vague triangle, clouded by mistrust between friends and suspicion of non-platonic motives weighed upon his troubled mind. It was all very much like daytime TV. But if he cast me as a latter day Socrates, in an effort to fathom Floyd's platonism with Jane, he belabored my role, which was far simpler, unless husbanding a shrew to rival Xantippe put me in Socrates' league. I was a bit part player.

My scene in the movie was toward the middle. I kept watching for it, because it was over so fast. Astounded by the fact that the movie was still in circulation although it made no concession whatever to the dictums of plot, in my heart, I was both angry and sad to hear the piffling dialog; angry at myself for not making better films when I was able, and frustrated because I had written immeasurably better screenplays that were never made into films.

Tensions unrelated to the film were percolating in several quadrants. The lovely Jane was jittery, her bursts of laughter somehow strained. Not drinking, for her, was not as difficult as watching Lyle Stone drink. He made her nervous with his brooding and mumbling.

Floyd and Annette had discovered each other. They were discussing delta blues music. In general, Floyd argued, wasn't it so that black people decried the Uncle Tomism purportedly inherent in that kind of music? He asked her to defend the position, as he understood it, of blacks embarrassed by the blues.

She insisted that he misunderstood the reasons why blues music currently was taking a back seat to rap and jazz among modern young blacks. The issue had more to do, she said, with the association of blues with racism, and the fact that the old ways that once were valid methods of dealing with it were no longer perceived as valid by today's standards.

"Do you like rap better?"

"Different forms have different structures. Rap represents a breaking away from the old forms, the old traditions that grew out of submission and subservience and reaches further back to the prouder cultural traditions of Africa, which is a distinction you, as a white man, may or may not recognize as critical to the black psyche. However, I assure you, it's an important consideration in relation to your question and, as such, cannot be overemphasized."

"But do you like it?" he asked.

"I prefer jazz," she smiled. "But I like all kinds of music."

"Do you prefer rap to blues?"

"That's not a fair question," she said.

"Why not? Either you do or you don't."

She gave him a cool look and refused to answer.

"Far be it from me to interrupt a good conversation," I said, "but my scene's coming up. There. There I am."

Jane gasped. "Look at you, Pete."

There I was, striding across a set stage in my incredibly handsome former life. A few short lines and I was gone.

"That's it?" said Lyle. "Play it back."

"Hey, Pete," said Huckie, "that was you?"

"In the flesh."

"What were you, about twenty-five?" said Lyle.

"Twenty-three, I think."

The scene played again. "There I go," I thought. There I went.

There was no sadness in the scene, and only admiration in my friends' reactions, but it was a little wrenching to watch that one short ludicrous scene replayed, knowing it was the culmination of a young actor's dreams.

Like a mindreader, Lyle exchanged my empty glass for a full one. "Hey, bartender," I said. He grinned and turned a robust thumb up.

I sipped my drink and watched the rest of the film from a distant place where all my sons were with me and we were watching together the first of the many movies I had made over a long and prolific career.

Between films, we filled our paper plates with an assortment of picnic items; baked beans and burgers and coleslaw and homemade potato salad. Chips and dip.

"The next one's more interesting," I said.

"Tough act to follow," said Floyd.

"This one's in color."

As the credits for *The Brides Wore Blood* began to roll, I recalled that it was my good friend, Larry Graham, who introduced me to Lee Jennings. In those days, Jenny and I attended many social functions sponsored by the paper. Larry and I were great friends then. He was still a working journalist and was about to begin writing the great novel about Vietnam he always talked about. He knew everyone at the party and was quick to import any worthwhile gossip to me, his pal of pals.

"There's a movie producer in the crowd tonight," he said, in the low voice he reserved for confidential matters. "Can you pick him out?"

I gave the party the once over. "Give me a hand, Lar, there are about a hundred people here."

He shifted his position and diddled the ice in his glass. He'd seen too many spy movies. Feigning a crafty whisper, he said, "The blonde in the orange dress to your left."

"Her?"

"No, the squirrely guy with her. Lee Jennings. He's from Myrtle Beach, my old hometown. Won't remember me, but I know the boy. He made a few skinflicks, now he's legit. Not wealthy, but he gets things done."

"Lead on, Lar."

He was right. Lee Jennings didn't remember him, but that meant nothing to Larry Graham. He made a play for Lee's wife and led her away while I talked t o Lee about film.

That's how it was back then with Larry. Newly divorced, he became the bachelor writer, the hound, the lion, the carousing literary roue. Ten years later, he had a thousand pages scattered on the floor of his study, and two empty quart bottles of vodka on his desk. I picked up the unnumbered manuscript pages, collated them and stacked them away in a safe place. Then I picked him up, not for the first time, by any means, and put him to bed.

When he decided to marry again, this time to a teetotaler, he used to come to my house to hide out. Madge would call and I would lie to her for him. He was slumped in a chair in my living room where he'd been for two days straight, sleeping it off, but I told her no, I had not seen him.

Little things like that a woman never forgets. So I was persona non grata in her house, though she tolerated me sometimes. Larry was no better than a kept man in that marriage. She had the money. He didn't have to work. He spent ten more years on his novel.

Books about Vietnam flooded the market, but his just never quite ended. People talk about me and my script, but I knew and he knew he had nothing on me.

"Hey, Pete, wake up, we need a commentary here." Floyd's voice jogged me back to the present. "What the hell's going on here, you sleeping?"

"Leave him alone," said Jane, "maybe he's tired."

"Sorry," I said, "I just have a lot on my mind."

"Commentary, please," said Floyd.

"In this scene," I said, focusing again on the film, "the aged Count DeLorca is searching the occult library for a way to break the curse which has plagued his family for centuries. His son is a vampire, a congenital trait that skips generations, and is busy luring tourist women to the castle. One of them shall be his bride. The others will all be killed and drained of blood."

"Where do you come in?" asked Jane.

"When you see a mysterious pentagram on the basement floor, that's the beginning of my scene. I'm a dark force conjured from the underworld."

"That sounds cool," said Carol.

"This film has everything!" Annette laughed. "Voodoo too!"

I turned to Floyd and said, "You know, Henry's starting to dabble in voodoo."

"Voris' Henry?" His ears perked up. Floyd was keen on local gossip and relied on me to keep him up to date.

"Later," I said.

"Tell me now."

"Voris found a chicken head in her ashtray."

"A chicken head," Floyd repeated, "in her ashtray."

"Henry's campaign to get her to move appears to be working," I continued. "She's decided to have a yard sale."

"Where are they moving to?"

"Sanford. Why is the question. Why move at all, much less to Sanford?"

"Maybe I read too many murder books," said Floyd, "but if Henry really wanted to get rid of her, wouldn't he take her off someplace where nobody knew her, and nobody would miss her? Someplace like Sanford?"

"This sounds interesting," said Annette. "Who's Henry?"

To my mind, her question deserved an abridged version of Voris' story, or better yet, a long dissembling rant on an unrelated topic, but Floyd had no such qualms. He found the whole indelicate saga amusing.

"Mandingo and Maud," he said.

"Mandingo what?" Annette reacted with sudden tension.

"Voris and Henry," I interrupted Floyd's smug chuckle to say, "are the interracial, inter-generational couple of the neighborhood. He is her junior by thirty years. She is white. He is black."

"So?" Annette raised her eyebrows.

"He's forty something. She's seventy something," Floyd added.

"I still don't get it," said Annette. "Are you racist, or what?"

"Being concerned is not racist," I said. "When an elderly woman is taken advantage of by a pathetic individual, his color is of no importance whatever."

"What if she's happy?" said Carol, out of the blue.

"If she's happy, fine. It's her money. If it makes her happy to spend a fortune on toys for his playroom, what concern is it of mine? Am I my neighbor's keeper?"

"If she was happy, she wouldn't want to move, would she?" said Carol, "not to Sanford."

"And you think he wants to kill her?" asked Annette.

I jerked a thumb at Floyd. "He said that."

She looked at him with evident distaste. "You believe that?"

He shrugged. "If they go to Sanford, we'll never see Voris again."

"That is a horrible thing to say. Do you even know the man?"

"No," said Floyd.

"On hearsay alone, you pass judgement on him. That's discrimination."

"You don't find it the least bit humorous, do you?" Floyd's puzzlement was tainted with sarcasm. "Why don't I just round up me a posse and go lynch his black ass. That'll learn him not to meddle with white women."

Annette was unamused. She looked around. "I don't know, Jane," she said. "They're your friends. I'm not about to defend this Henry guy, whoever he is, I just don't believe, if he was white, that he'd be automatically condemned."

"Women do tend to look for the good in people more than men," said Huckie, offering a profundity that gave us all a much needed pause.

Jane's pleasant demeanor took on the aspect of a mask. My personal bartender was busy whispering in her ear, so I stood to stretch my legs and wandered into the kitchen to help myself. An almost gloomy silence was settling over the room and the movie was not exciting enough to dispel it, until my scene began.

"There it is!" Jane cried, "The pentagram! Pete, you're on! You're on!"

I never tired of watching that scene. A line of chalk, a forty-nine cent smoke bomb, and presto, from the depths I rise, cloaked in an ominous black cape, my face, as slowly I turn, covered with a white gelatinous substance. What titanic special effects! I rubbed my cheeks recalling the phenomenal itch of the mask of caulk drying on my face.

"Commentary, please," Floyd requested.

"Ok, I've been conjured into the basement of the mansion and I serve no purpose in the film, except to summon the girls to their trysts with the vampire, Juan. Meanwhile, I do battle with the lover of one of the girls, who comes to her rescue. There he is now. Watch him take that big machete. Notice it's not fake. Lucky he didn't kill me with it. As you can see, the ghoul has no sword, nor does he possess any supernatural powers."

"Hell of a fight," said Lyle, as the ghoul grappled with the burly swordsman, knocking over tables and various rustic props.

"Eight minutes," I said. "Nothing like it in the annals of film. I was fighting for my life. The guy kept slashing at me. He got so carried away with his role he must have thought I was a real phantom. Then he cut me right below the eye and I got very angry. He was supposed to come at me like so and appear to run me through, the sword under the arm bit, I fall, and it's over. But he was left-handed and the camera was to his left, so I had to circle all the way around to the other side, then, I guess the machete got heavy and he switched hands. Finally, I got him in an armlock and was able to give him some stage directions."

"Do you remember what you said to him?" asked Jane.

"My exact words, I believe, were 'Die, you fool, but don't cut me again, or I'll break your arm.'"

"Wait a minute," said Lyle, "if you're a spirit, can he kill you with a sword?"

"Don't expect logic in this movie," I said.

"Wow," Jane gasped, as the fight scene ended. "That was fabulous. Did you make any other movies?"

"Not yet," I said.

The rest of the film plodded on toward its bloody climax. The storyline was one long tangle of clichés and incongruities. Despite my commentaries, a pervading sense of bafflement was the general reaction to the ending.

As the final credits rolled, I was the recipient of laudatory handshakes and unanimous goodwill. The warmth of their appreciation all but moved me to tears. I was unprepared for such a bath of affection.

Music again became the topic of conversation. Lyle began telling Annette about The Rubes.

"I'm getting us a gig," he said to Floyd.

Annette looked at Floyd with renewed interest.

"We all sing and write songs together," said Lyle.

"What kind of songs?" Annette asked.

"We're sort of a country doowop folk blues jug band," said Floyd.

"No rap?" Annette smiled.

"Not yet," said Floyd.

"I got us a gig on the deck at Mango's," said Lyle. "That's a beach bar." He informed Annette.

"You should take it," she said, "it's good experience."

"We're not ready for that," said Floyd.

"Playing in public builds confidence," she said.

"Yeah, Floyd," Lyle echoed.

The sound of an argument between Carol and Huckie arose from the far corner. "I'll hide your leg," she threatened.

"Like hell," said Huckie. "I can have a damn beer."

The phone ringing interrupted them and Jane sprang forth to answer it. Within moments, she was crying into the receiver and begging her teenage daughter to come home. When she hung up, she burst into tears.

"She's in love with a high school dropout!" she wailed. "Now she wants to quit school and marry him. God, what if she's pregnant?"

Into this melee of distractions rode Walter on his bicycle, with an important message for me. His bike crashed against the pavement, then he knocked on the door. I had half-expected him to show up after work. He didn't like to be left out of things.

"Hey, Pete," he called as he pounded on the glass. He was plastered.

"Who's that?" asked Annette.

"That's Walter," said Floyd.

"Is he in the band, too?"

"He is the band," said Floyd.

"I think I'm getting the picture," she said.

Jane was sobbing into a towel. "I can't handle Walter now. Lyle," she pleaded, "please, make him go away."

"What do you want me to do?" said Lyle. "Make him stand outside?"

"If you let him in, he'll never leave," Floyd warned.

"Floyd, please," said Jane, "get him to go home."

The pounding continued. "He'll break that glass," said Lyle.

"Please don't be rude to him," said Jane.

I opened the door and stepped outside. "Hi, Walter," I said.

"Pete," he said, "How you doing? You doing all right? Listen, I like you, Pete. You're tops with me. But you got to go home right away, and you got to move."

"Walter," I said, "be serious."

"The realtor called. The landlady's flying in from Arizona today. She's coming right now. You got to get out of that room."

"Today?" I said.

"Right now," he said. "She's on her way right now."

"Ok." I had to change gears.

Floyd joined us, closing the door behind him. "What's up?"

"I need to leave right away. Can you put his bike in your van?"

"Sure."

"Hey, you got a party going on?" said Walter.

"The party's over," said Floyd. "Come on, Walt, I'll give you a ride home."

"I don't want to go home," said Walter. He pushed past Floyd and began to pound on the glass door again. "Hey, what are you, having a party or something?"

Floyd tried to pull him away from the door, but Walter planted his feet, inviting brute force to try and move him.

"You don't like me, do you?" he said.

"Walter," said Floyd, "don't start that."

"Walt," I said, "let's get the bike in the van."

Walter pounded on the glass again, ignoring us.

Then Jane flung the door open and rushed out in a screaming fit telling Walter to leave before she called the police and waving her arms as if to frighten or shoo him away. When she ran out of hysterical threats and gestures, she burst into tears again and went back inside.

Lyle came out with a beer in his hand, oblivious to all the commotion. "What's happening?"

Walter had backed up but still stood rooted. "I didn't do nothing wrong," he said.

Floyd took hold of the bicycle and rolled it out to the van. He fitted it in through the side and slid the door shut. "Come on, Walt," he said, "let's go home."

Walter focused one eye on Floyd, then trudged across the yard to the van. "I didn't do nothing wrong," he repeated. He was unresistant as we backed him into the van.

"Walter," I said, "are you sure the realtor said today?"

"I didn't do nothing wrong," he repeated it like a litany. "I didn't do nothing wrong."

Chapter Seventeen
The Queen of the Georgia Package,
or "Et tu, Lar?"

My mind was numb. On the short ride home, I clung to the last vain shreds of hope; that Walter had misinterpreted the message, that my residency was salvageable, that reason and justice would yet prevail. Though it was second nature to me to plan alternative strategies, I kept a rein on that reflex, denying to the last the prospect of losing my little place.

Time was short. As soon as Floyd pulled into his yard, Katie leaned out of her door and called, "Have you seen Wall?"

Floyd slid the side door open and Walter climbed out. Katie came across the yard, speaking in a panicked tone.

"The realtor's coming over with the owner right now. If she sees you drunk, Wall, she won't sell us the house."

Walter said, "I'm not drunk, Kate."

"Just let me talk to her, Wall," said Katie. "Pete, you got to get your stuff out of there. She's on her way over right now."

Floyd lifted Walter's bike out and closed the van. He went inside, leaving Walt and Katie talking in his front yard. I walked over to my little place with a heavy heart.

A few minutes later, Walter rode off on his bicycle in the general direction of the liquor store. I had not yet begun to pack when a beige Lincoln pulled in the driveway and parked right outside my open door. A woman with a pugnacious glower, who could only have been Mrs. Halloran's daughter emerged from the back seat and marched into my room.

"And who might you be?" she demanded.

"Peter Foster," I said. "You must be Alberta. The family resemblance is striking. I often assisted your mother in various ways."

"My mother's in the nuthouse where she belongs," she growled. "Who said you could live here? What kind of rent are you paying them?"

"Rent? Oh, no, dear, I've been visiting for a couple of days here. The Wellingtons were kind enough to put me up while my son's apartment building is being fumigated. He lives a few blocks away, on Eighth Avenue."

"Just pack your things and vamoose. This apartment's not theirs to let out."

She turned to the realtor, a quiet little bald fellow, lingering in the doorway, and said, "Keep an eye on him."

"See here," I said, that's hardly necessary."

"Mister, just get on with it. I don't have time to argue with you."

"There's no need to be rude," I said. I looked to the realtor for a reaction. He consulted his watch and looked up at the sky. Alberta rapped on the adjoining door until Katie opened it. She went in to talk with her.

I finished packing and set my bags on the porch for the moment. Then I headed over to Floyd's. He was sitting on his front steps, sipping a glass of red wine.

As I passed under the cypress branches that bordered the two yards, I heard a rustle above my head as a fish fell through the branches and landed with a thud in the grass by my feet. In the blue sky above, an osprey was winging away while a lone mockingbird darted back and forth above the tree.

"Did you see that?" said Floyd. "The mockingbird attacked the osprey and made him drop the fish. Looks like it landed in my yard.

If I were prone to omen divination, I'd say that didn't bode well. Such an omen might mean that a burden of some sort is about to drop into my domain."

"Could be a good omen," I said, "how often does a fish fall out of the sky?"

"When you get around to mowing the lawn, you'll move it, won't you?"

"I certainly will," I said.

He made room for me on the steps and we sat in silence watching the cars go by. I lit a cigarette, and waited.

"Don't even say it, Pete," he said. "Don't even think it. You can stay tonight, maybe tomorrow night, but you can't move in. Find something else, Pete. Don't push it this time."

"Ok, kid."

The phone rang. He jumped up to answer it. "It's for you," he said, coming back outside. "Frances."

"Wonder what she wants," I said.

She was calling from the hospital, where she was recovering from major surgery. "Pete," she said, sounding very weak, "I've been gunshot."

By her voice, I had no doubt that she was serious.

"Four slugs." Her whisper creaked like an ancient hinge. "Sorry to bother you, Pete. Doctor says I'll pull through, but I'm tired. Real tired. Want to ask you one favor. I'll be getting out in a couple of days, maybe. Will you check on Mr. Delbert for me? See if he's all right?"

"Of course, Frances. Don't worry about a thing. My God, four bullets?"

Her breath was labored. "They're doping me up, now, Pete. I got to go. You'll do that for me, won't you? You're a good friend, Pete. You need to come by more. I'll cook you a meal you won't forget."

"I'll take care of it, Frances."

I put down the receiver wondering if Delbert knew, or if he had noticed yet that she was gone. "Check on Delbert," she had said. And I had agreed, so that was my next mission. Things were moving kind of fast, but I was handling it. I could deal with Delbert for a couple of days.

"Kid," I said, as I stepped back outside. "I've got an errand to run for Frances. I may not be back tonight. If not, we're still talking two days, right? Forty-eight hours, not necessarily consecutive?"

"Just do what you have to do, Pete," he said. "I'll leave the side door open."

"Thanks, kid." I started walking down to Delbert's.

I hadn't been there for a while. The fence was still not finished. Not that it mattered. If I ever did finish it would be time to start over again.

Delbert was inside in front of the tube, in his chair, in his underwear. He was holding his bowed head in his hands. He looked up when I knocked. I waved to him through the front porch window.

"Pete," he said. "That you, Pete?"

"It's me, Delbert."

"Frances is dead," he blurted.

"She's not dead, Delbert. I just talked to her. She's in the hospital. She'll be home in a couple days."

"She will?" He picked up the remote control and started flipping channels. "I thought she was dead."

"Who told you that, Delbert?"

He shrugged, perplexed by the question. "A lady called. Said she was shot."

"She's recovering nicely. I don't know the details. She asked me to see how you were getting along. Do you need anything?"

"Beer," he said. His thumb kept clicking through channels. "Nothing good on," he muttered.

"Ok, beer. Anything else?"

He grunted and scratched himself. "Food."

"Ok, food." I went through the motions of making a list. "Give me some money and I'll go to the store."

He shook his big head. "No money."

"No money, no beer, no food," I said.

"Alright, Goddamn, alright!" he exploded, jumping up and tearing down the hallway. "sheesh!"

While he was gone I glanced at some of the photos and artifacts in frames on one wall. A plaque commending Delbert for bravery at sea. A photo of a much younger Delbert in a Santa Claus suit with a child on his knee. A small photo of a young soldier fading in its frame. I guessed that to be Frances' son.

Delbert returned with his wallet. I hoped he wasn't going to go through the ritual of throwing it on the carpet. Apparently, his momentary huff had passed, leaving no trace. He riffled through several small bills, licking his thumb like a bank clerk, pulled out a twenty and handed it to me. "Frances not dead?" he said. "No shit?"

"She's fine," I said. "She'll be home in a day or two." I started for the door.

"Where you going?"

"To the store."

"You coming back?"

"Of course, I'm coming back."

"Ok, Pete." He settled back in his chair again with the remote control. "Get some beer."

I closed the door behind me. The air outside that house was sweet. I lit a cigarette and took a few steps toward the road. Then I remembered Frances' senior citizen vehicle. The big tricycle was up against the side of the house. I wheeled it around, checked the air in the tires, climbed on and started pedaling. As long as I was in the neighborhood, it seemed like a good idea at the time to stop by Larry Graham's. He only lived a couple of blocks over.

Madge's car was gone. That was a good sign. He answered my knock in his bathrobe. It was just getting dark. He did not look pleased to see me.

"Hey, Lar," I said. "How goes it?"

He put on his Hemingway scowl and unlatched the door. "I suppose you've come to drink my liquor," he said. His voice had a surly edge.

I wasn't offended by his gruff manner. It was part of his charm.

With a mocking gesture he indicated that I knew where it was and why not help myself. Larry had been warned by his doctor to stop drinking or die. He had cut down enormously, but his cabinet was still well stocked. I knew where everything was.

"Nothing for me, thanks," he grumbled.

I poured a modest glass of his finest vodka over ice and joined him in the living room.

"What's on your mind, Pete?" he said, without interest. He was in one of his get-to-the-point moods.

"As of today, I'm homeless again."

"Oh, for Christ sake, Pete, I thought you were set."

"There's been a new development. The sudden return of the absentee landlady."

"Why do I not want to hear this?" he groaned.

"Not to worry, Lar. A minor setback."

"I can't help you, Pete."

"Larry, did I ask you for anything? You're my oldest friend. I wouldn't dream of imposing on your sterling hospitality."

"Don't start on me, Pete. I'm not in the mood."

"Larry, it's Pete. Remember me? Enough with the Hemingway bit. Your moods don't concern me. I know how it is with you and Madge. You've got a nice pad here, office, desk, books, attractive furnishings, soft couch. You've come a long way since I pulled you out of the gutter."

"You ever think of checking into detox, Pete? Could be it might do you some good."

"Did it do you any good?" I said.

"Helped me to see myself as others saw me."

"You mean as a puffed up pseudo intellectual? That must have been quite a catharsis."

He favored me with a wan smile. "You're baiting me, Pete. You don't have the ammo."

I rattled the ice in my glass. "Oh, not?"

"Maybe I will have one drink," he said, with a trace of his old grand courtly manner. "Would you care for another?"

I gave him my glass. He refilled it for me and returned to his chair with a large shot glass full of bourbon, neat, which he sipped and placed on a decorative cork coaster on the end table. He smiled an empty smile, his eyes humorless and predatory.

"News on Caminiti?" he asked.

Same old tact. Big me little you. "He's making progress."

"How long has he had it, a year now? What is that, Hollywood time?"

Bored with his petulance, I waved it aside. "Is that your best shot? What have you been writing for the last twenty years? You're at least two wars behind, Lar. The Falklands, Grenada, the Middle East. Where's Larry? What's left to say about Vietnam?"

"Nothing. So what? Your script's still not happening, Pete. At best, it's a pastiche of incongruent subtleties."

"Pastiche? Well, now. Pierced by the rapier."

He slid a little deeper into his chair. "I wish you well, Pete, but our years of friendship don't obligate me to take an indulgent view of your script. If something comes of it, fine, but I wouldn't hold my breath if I were you."

"You think it's derivative?"

"Of course it is. Every colossal turd is derivative." He held up a palm, "yes, even mine, especially mine. Granted, your script has some brilliant scenes, but taken as a whole, it's unwieldy and dated and overwritten to the point of insanity."

Larry had good booze.

"Well, what else you got going, a little painting here and there?"

"I manage to keep my hand in the trade."

"But, as of today, you're homeless." He looked around the room. "I do all the painting here myself."

I drained my drink and set the glass down on a coaster. "Larry," I said, "give Madge my regards."

He didn't get up. I climbed on the tricycle and pedaled off to run Delbert's errand.

On the way, I stopped by Arthur's, to see which way the wind was blowing. He and Bradley were quarreling over money. As I entered, Bradley stormed out and slammed the heavy door.

Arthur looked at me, reading in my expression of dismay, a confirmation. "Well, Dad," he said, "on the road again, are you?"

"Arthur, please," I said.

"Dad, I need Brad's half of the rent. If he moves out, which he's threatening to do, I can't handle this place alone. I'll have to get a roommate. How can I get a roommate with you here? Brad won't stay if you're here, that's the bottom line."

"A couple of days." I said.

"Dad, I've got a hard decision to make. I don't want to hurt you, but I can't go on like this."

"Like what?"

"Like this, damn it!" He was close to tears.

"Arthur, what? What are you talking about?"

"If I Myers Act you, Dad, they'll put you through detox, then you'll come under the social services rehab program. They'll take care of you."

I was shocked. "I wasn't aware that I needed to be taken care of. This is Larry's idea. You've been talking to Larry."

He nodded. "And to Mom. The subject's come up several times. I didn't want to push the idea as long as you were functioning."

"Since when am I not functioning? Oh, this is rich. Larry thinks I should be detoxified. What do you think, son? Never mind what Larry or your mother thinks. What do you think?"

"Dad," a tear fell when he said the word, "how can you go on the way you're living? Maybe it's not the right answer, but I don't see any other way."

"You don't see any other way?"

"Not unless you have a place to live, other than here. You can't live with Floyd?"

"He's not my family," I said.

"I'm sorry, Dad," he said.

"Look, give me a couple of days to see what I can come up with. I'll find something. If not, I'll do as you say. For you, Arthur, not for me. If you want me in detox, I'll go. But I'm disappointed that you let Larry influence your thinking. This is no solution. This is a delay."

"You'll call me in a couple of days, then?"

"No," I said. "I'll be at Floyd's. You can call there, or leave a message."

Regardless of my feelings, I still had an errand to run. Delbert was the last person on earth I felt like seeing next, but the thought of him in his underwear waiting for me to return with beer and food, his eyes alternating at regular intervals between the clock and The Flintstones, was a hard one to ignore. So I pedaled the tricycle to the grocery store and bought frozen pizzas and beer for Delbert and some cigarettes for myself. I pocketed the change, about four bucks, put the groceries in a basket and pedaled off into the night again.

At Delbert's the phone rang. Frances calling. "She keeps calling," said Delbert, "you talk to her." He traded the phone for the bag of groceries, from which he extracted one beer with gusto and left the bag on the floor by the television, forgotten for the moment.

"Reckon I'm not so easy to kill," Frances said, with a renewed sense of garrulity. "They can't keep me under, either. They done give me every drug they got. I keep waking up. So, what the hell, I guess I'm going to make it, Pete. Thanks for looking out for Mr. Delbert. You were gone a long time, though. Where'd you get off to? Oh, never mind. You want to know what happened? Well, I was all dolled up in the Georgia Package Friday night, took a cab up there and was having a drink, not bothering a soul. You know how the bar is, in a circle. Well, a man on the other side of the bar leaned over at me with a .22 pistol in his hand and he didn't say one word, just shot me, bam, four times. Like to killed me. Missed my heart and all my vital organs. Wasn't no shot, was he? Ha. Pete, it's a damn shame when you can't even have a drink at the GP without being shot at. They sent me flowers, Mary and the folks down there, a nice get well card everybody signed. They won't see me back there any too soon. Reckon I'll be staying pretty close to home from here on. Most of the time, anyhow. You still there, Pete?"

"Right here, Frances."

"What you think of that? Ha. Put Delbert back on. I'm going to ream him out some, put the fear of God in him, get him to clean up the house a little. Doc wants for me to stay in bed at least a week. I'll have some work for you, too, soon as I'm fit to supervise. Anyhow, thanks, Pete, you're a good man to help out like you did. See you later."

I passed the phone to Delbert and left, taking the tricycle.

Exhausted at the end of my day, I parked it in Floyd's side yard and went in the kitchen door.

Floyd was out. I went up to my room and fell on the mattress like a stone.

In the morning, I brought Floyd up to date on my developing situation. As expected, he remained unmoved.

"If I'm your only alternative," he said, "you have no alternative."

Another time, I might have felt tempted to press the issue with Floyd. Another time, I might have felt hurt by his recalcitrance. This time, I felt stoic and serene about the eventual outcome. The absurdity of submitting myself to a detox unit at first made me very angry but I gradually began to see not only the irony, but the tactical logic of submission. To resist was futile and proved nothing. To endure the indignity without complaint would demonstrate to Arthur more vividly than any resistance the reserves of my character.

With Christlike patience, I waited that day and most of the next for the phone call, which eventually came. Arthur was on his way.

He arrived with Larry in Larry's car. Like a lamb I walked to the car and climbed into the back seat. Arthur looked me in the eye and said, "Thanks, Dad." Larry tried to be jolly, but I wasn't having any. I did my stonefaced impression of Buster Keaton the entire way in.

Chapter Eighteen
Detox or Delay

During my fifteen days in detox I never felt less like an alcoholic.
All around me were people with real problems; junkies, crack addicts, sterno drinkers. In relative terms, I had more in common with the Dalai Lama, or the Pope.

Withdrawal symptoms were not part of my experience, no delirium tremens, not even the slightest physical discomfort. Fifteen days without a drink was nothing, a walk in the park.

In any city, the regimen of institutions is much the same. Dregs of society are herded in like cattle and processed with no regard for individual circumstances. My insistence on keeping my typewriter with me was considered a most unusual request, which sent the staff into a quandary and was only granted after a halfhearted attempt to pry it from my grip.

Cast into the throng of pitiful addicts and victims and blubbering human refuse, I was one of the few not crying or cursing or threatening to commit unspeakable acts.

No sooner was I shown to my quarters than I set up the typewriter on my cot and began to make a productive use of my time. Aware, as days passed, of quizzical looks cast my way by both the staff and other detainees, more than once I heard the whispers, "Mr. Foster, he so strange man. Why he here?" Oblivious to their curiosity, I found my powers of concentration were such that not even the glaring lack of privacy in the dayroom daunted me. I wrote long letters to faraway friends, outlined alternative plans for the script, in the event that Caminiti's efforts didn't pan out. Also, an idea for a new screenplay began to take shape in my mind. I made notes and started observing some of the other detainees more closely. Without question, there was a surfeit of depressing material in the room, a sinkhole of human tragedies, an overabundance of nightmarish characters, and so little that was comical.

There was one old man who had been there twelve times. He had an amusing outlook. "When I get out of here," he said, "I will go straight downtown to Junior's bar and have a drink. Pick up right where I left off." With his white whiskers a twinkle in his eye, he grinned like a deranged Santa Claus. "And do you know why, Mister Pete? Can you tell me why, sir?"

He waited for an answer to his rhetorical question. "Because it's there? Because you must? Because a man must do what a man must do? Why, sir? Why, indeed?"

He leaned forward to whisper the secret. "Because why not?" he said. "That one question stumps me every single time."

His name was Willy, and he wore the mantle of a patriarch among the detainees. His vast institutional experience provided an invaluable human resource to the rank and file. He spent hours answering scores of specific questions regarding the maze of forms and signatures required for early release and various visiting privileges. Knowledge of the ins and outs of the system had secured him a singular position of respect. He was the man with the answers, the padrone.

As a result of my association with him, it was assumed by some that I, too, was privy to the bureaucracy's arcane esoterics. Nothing could be further from the truth. Had I known the secrets of early release, would I not have utilized them in my own behalf?

The answer to that question surprised me. The fact to face was that I had no place to go. Once my fifteen days were up, I would need a plan of action. Never mind the long term plan, my short term options took precedence.

Maybe the money was still in the piano. Alberta Halloran deserved no less a comeuppance for her rudeness. With courage aplenty now, I had no qualms about bringing in a partner, Walter or Floyd, perhaps both of them, the more the merrier. We all needed the money. But that was in the abstract realm, to come later, after extensive planning.

On the tangible side of the ledger, there was Henry's grandiose scheme of a wholesale electronics empire. Whether or not it could ever be made to work was immaterial. He was chomping at the bit to get his ad campaign off the ground. I'd kept him dangling long enough with mild encouragements. Now, he and Voris were moving. That, in itself, opened up a range of opportunities. For one, the house would be vacant, and who better to house sit than her husband's business partner, the Southeast Regional Sales Manager?

Yes, the time had come to hone in on the Goodnights. Floyd needed a break from me. By Christmas, he'd be more amenable. Frances was always good for an odd job. She owed me now, and I could finish her fence anytime. Larry Graham was off my list for good. As for Arthur, I only hoped that he would understand someday that everything I ever did or tried to do was for his sake, and Bradley's. If I was doomed to live without my sons' respect, it was a fate I did not deserve and could only deny to my last breath. Nothing else in my life had any meaning if I lost that battle.

I went to sleep at night with the muffled, writhing sounds of agonized deprivation all around me. Yea, though I walk through the valley, I prayed. And day by day, I felt my strength of purpose renewed and verified. In the back of my mind, one word fed my will with hope. Excelsior: Ever Upward.

When Willy was released, the magisterial essence of his authority passed to me like an invisible baton, and though I continued to deny having any special knowledge of forms, my protests fell on deaf ears. Like Solomon, I relied on common sense and cryptic instinct. As for forms, I found that I had absorbed enough of the basics from Willy to fulfill my role as padrone pro tem.

The day I was released, they were readmitting Willy. A dog

had bitten him on the ear and the side of his head was bandaged. His face was a bright and dangerous red. On the whole, he looked considerably less cheerful than he did on the day of his release. Our eyes met in the hall and we slowed our walks as we passed each other. I saluted him and he mustered a wink.

"Thirteen's a charm," he said, as the male attendant pushed him forward through the double doors.

No one knew I was released that day. No one was home when I made my calls. I had a bus schedule in my wallet and a couple of bucks for the fare. I found a bus stop and sat on my suitcase to wait. After several transfers and about a five mile walk, I made it back to Floyd's.

A blonde woman with a sunny smile answered his door. Her high Nordic cheekbones and glinting, bright blue-eyes looked familiar. My immediate feeling was that we had met somewhere before, perhaps long ago, but I could not place her. She held the screen door open for me to slide my bags up onto the porch. "You must be Pete," she said, with the warmth of a hostess. "I'm Viola Henley. Come in."

Chapter Nineteen
Voris' Chest or "Which Mrs. Ferguson?"

She very graciously offered me a chair. I took a load off and appraised the situation. The living room looked no different. The same protective layer of dust still coated every object. The oval coffee table in front of the couch still had its quota of magazines and papers strewn in disarray across its expanse. No cleaning or straightening up had yet been done, but there were signs that she was contemplating the need for drastic measures.

Her hands, as she sat on the couch opposite me, fidgeted with the scattered magazines, arranging them in neat stacks. Floyd, she said, was gone to see about some work and should be back soon. I looked around in vain for an ashtray.

"Would you like a drink of water or something?" she asked with a honeyed smile. She rose and started for the kitchen, hands poised to perform a kindly service. As she inspected the glasses in the cupboard with distaste for the hard water film, I felt the bristling portent of a changing wind, whispering caveats through the hallowed halls of the Deadbeat Hotel.

I was reminded of the Spanish proverb regarding the seasonal Solano wind, "Ask no favor during the Solano." The presaging breeze intimated what anyone with eyes could see; Miss Viola was not one to accept the status quo.

She brought me water in a sparkling glass. I thanked her and began to relate, at her request, some of my recent experiences downtown. I obliged her with an anecdote or two and found her to be a delightful listener as well as an engaging conversationalist. We passed a comfortable hour getting acquainted. Then Walter came to the door.

"Oh, no," Viola sighed. She looked at me. "I won't let him in while Floyd's gone."

"Not to worry," I said. "I'll take care of him." I stepped outside. "Hello, Walter."

"Pete," he said with surprise, "how are you, bud?"

Viola followed onto the porch and watched through the screen door. Walter leered up at her. "Hello, Viola," he said, "you lovely creature."

"Hi, Walter," she responded.

"Come on out," said Walter. "Don't be shy."

She came down the steps. Walter put an arm across her shoulder and grinned. "How do you like my new girlfriend, Pete? Isn't she adorable?"

"Without a doubt," I said.

She twisted out of his grasp, fanning the air. "Whew, Walter, that drink smells awful."

"Want a sip?" said Walter.

"Pass," said Viola.

"How about you, Pete? Want a drink?"

"Walter, no," said Viola, "he just got out of detox!"

"No kidding," said Walter. "Think he's thirsty? What about it, Pete? Feel like a drink?"

Walter was not inclined to notice any subtle signals of mine to nix that line of conversation.

"Not right now," I said.

Disapproval hung like a cloud over Viola's pale features. "You should be ashamed of yourself," she said to Walter. "And Pete, if you take a drink, I'll be so disappointed. I don't think Floyd will be too happy, either, if it turns out that you don't have any more willpower than that."

There it was, the voice of authority. "I've no intention of drinking with Walter," I said. "Actually, I have other business to attend to, thank you." I couldn't help but be a little riled by her tone. On whose behalf did she presume to scold me? Whence arose such temerity? But argument would have been counterproductive. Let what winds there may be blow, I could hold my tongue.

I resolved to move on toward the Goodnights. Let Floyd draw his own conclusions from the red suitcase and the typewriter on his porch.

"Tell Floyd I'll be in touch."

She stepped back into the house as I started walking away, oblivious to Walter's echoing call.

"Pete, come back, Pete. Hey, Pete."

I felt like Shane.

At Voris' house, a moving van was loading up her possessions. She and Henry greeted me like a long lost cousin and asked me to stay for dinner. Voris gave me a cigarette. Her hand shook as she snapped her lighter.

Henry excused himself and returned to his computer room where he was engaged in the process of disconnection.

"So," I said, "you're really moving."

"We're moving," she nodded, as a pair of uniformed movers carried out a bureau. "Tomorrow."

"If there's anything I can do to help, Voris," I said, "anything at all."

"There is," she said. "Henry needs you."

"Needs me? In what capacity?"

She blew a stream of smoke at the table and waved through it with her hand. "He needs some help with his business. He wants you to help him write an ad or something."

"I can do that."

"Also," she lowered her voice and tilted her head toward mine, "he doesn't have any friends. Will you be his friend, Pete?"

She looked at me with a bizarre and desperate longing in her red rimmed eyes. "I have to leave my plants here, Pete." She gripped my arm. "No room down there for plants, he says."

"Would you like me to keep an eye on things while you're gone? I am an experienced house-sitter."

"I'm sure you are, Pete." She sighed and touched a rubber tree leaf. "We listed with a realtor, already. We'll lock it up, I guess, until it's rented."

"You're not going to have the yard sale?"

"What yard sale? We're leaving tomorrow."

"What about your plants?"

"Henry can't be bothered with them," she said. "My lord and master."

"I'm sure he has more important things on his mind," I agreed.

"Yeah, like spending my money. I wish he'd go back to that concrete jungle where he came from."

Her fingers clenched on my arm like a lifeline. She wavered on the brink of an emotional display.

"That's something I can do for you, Voris, manage a yard sale. Pick up a little extra cash for you, see that your plants are well tended."

"You don't need to go through all that trouble," she said.

"No trouble. Besides, you might want to keep tabs on things while you are gone. You can call me and I'll keep you up to date."

"Let me talk to Henry about that," she said. "He may not like the idea, but I don't want my plants to die. I'd rather you found them all good homes."

"I can try."

"Henry!" she called.

He lumbered into the kitchen. "What?"

"What do you think about Pete holding a yard sale for us? That way he could sell some of my plants and some of these other things we need to get rid of."

He narrowed his eyes at me and grinned, "You wouldn't hold any of the money back for yourself?"

"Maybe a couple of bucks for cigarettes."

He laughed. "I think we can trust him."

"Of course, we can," said Voris.

"You'll need a list," said Henry, "of all the items and prices for everything. Don't let nobody talk you down."

Voris closed her eyes and rubbed her temples with her thumbs. "Whatever he says, Pete," she said, "just go along with him. It's all you can do."

At dinner, we discussed business and the importance of maintaining constant contact. Not for nothing had Henry installed a state-of-the-art telecommunications system. From their new home in Sanford, he would be able to call once a day on a toll-free circuit, leave a short recorded message for me to act upon, and never have to pay a dime unless I actually spoke into the phone. In the event that I might have a message for him, there was a way to reverse the system. Actual conversations were expensive, however, and to be avoided.

The ad that he wanted me to help him with was already written. He didn't want me to change, add or delete anything, just "punch it up a little." I told him it might take a few days and that my fee would be a hundred bucks. He whistled, but he liked to talk about large sums of money. His eyes glistened dreamily.

We agreed to meet in a week. He and Voris would return the following Saturday to pick me up and take me to their suite at the Hilton. We would hold our meeting there and iron out the details of our agreement. Why the Hilton? I did not even ask. Henry seemed to think it was a fine idea. As the night grew long, he grew more and more expansive.

"Cheap motels are all right for every day affairs," he said, "but for a dynamic undertaking such as ours, a little elegance and style is in order. A taste of things to come."

That night, they made their bed on some cushions, in a corner of their newly vacant bedroom. I found a place on the floor, where the couch used to be.

In the morning, Henry produced the list of yard sale items and prices. It was divided into two columns, things to sell and things not to sell. Hastily compiled, it was far from comprehensive. Only the lawnmower, his tools, and the piano were definitely not to be sold.

The piano, an antique upright, was an heirloom once belonging to Voris' mother. She had paid to have it tuned, but no one played. It sat against a wall in the emptied den, a relic of a bygone age, when there was music in the house.

"If it was up to me," said Henry, "I'd sell every damn thing. Might get a grand for the piano alone."

"No," said Voris, "no, no, no!"

The piano was definitely not to be sold.

On the sell list were plants, none priced at less than twelve dollars, assorted kitchen equipment, also priced in the stratosphere, some knickknacks and figurines that might catch an odd collector's eye, and several boxes of hardback books that once graced the long shelves of Ray Fletcher's library. There were no bargains. Henry figured the total value of all goods to be sold was six hundred and eighty dollars.

"Henry doesn't get out much," said Voris, perusing the list. "He's never even been to a yard sale."

We walked through the house and garage one last time before they left. There was still a considerable lot of merchandise, especially in the garage. Voris sighed. With a wave of her hand, she dismissed it all. "Just sell whatever you can, Pete. But not my piano. And not this either." She gently kicked a dark wooden chest by the door to the garage. It was overturned, the legs broken. "That's my cedar chest. I want it."

I added it to the list of items not to be sold.

Mastering the security system was the final hurdle. Unwilling to divulge the secret code, Henry instead showed me a way to disengage one door from the system by unplugging two little wires prior to leaving the house, which allowed one side door to open and close without setting off the alarm. My preference would have been to disengage the whole system, but at least I was able to get in and out without alerting the police. Each door and window had its own individualized buzzer identifying the point of entry. The house was like a minimum security prison. For a week I was to be both the warden and its sole inmate.

After a number of false starts and hesitations, the Goodnights finally pulled out of the drive and headed for Sanford. I found an interesting book in one of the boxes, took it and a tall drink of ice water out to the patio table in the shade and read in luxurious peace for several hours.

Henry had parted with a ten dollar advance for me to use to place an ad for a yard sale in the local paper. Yard sale signs with arrows placed on strategic street corners were another tried and true method. Even better, and less troubling, was the best advertising of all, word of mouth.

I gave Floyd a call and invited him over, asked him to bring my things. He arrived with many questions, and as we strolled through the vacant house, I explained the situation to him. First, he found the books, and winnowed through the boxes seeking titles to his liking. Then he spotted the piano.

"Is this for sale?" he asked, with instant desire.

"She won't part with it."

His hands roved over the filigreed carvings, his fingers tracing the delicate lines. "Mahogany," he said. "What a piece this would be refinished!"

I guided him away from it and onward down the hall. "A lot of this stuff is for sale. All the plants you saw out front."

"Don't want any plants," he said.

"Viola might. By the way, she's a lovely woman. If I put an ad in the paper, you see, then I'll have to stay here all the time. Whereas, if I know when someone is coming, I can arrange to be here at a certain time. You follow me?"

"You want me to help you unload some of this stuff, is that it?"

"For a fair price. I thought you'd appreciate having first shot at it."

"How much for the lawnmower?"

"Not for sale."

"Well, what is? Books and plants so far, what else?"

Then his eye fell upon the cedar chest, in blackened ruins overturned. "How about this, Pete?" He jerked it out from under the rakes and shovels that rested on it, so quickly claiming it that denial would have been a cruelty. "The legs are broken off or chipped. They can be fixed. The veneer is separated on top. That's not good, but I can do something with it. How much, Pete? Don't tell me it's not for sale."

As a moral issue, it might not have stymied the man of the cloth. But in the world of situational ethics, no hard and fast rules apply every time. "Ten bucks," I said. "I'll deal with Voris."

"What, she didn't want to sell it?"

"Don't worry," I said. "She probably won't even notice it's gone. If she does, I'll think of something. Mrs. Ferguson bought it. Don't give it another thought."

"I can make this chest look right," he said.

"Hey, and don't I know it? Kid, you've been good to me. And she's not all there anyway. Forget about it. What else do you see?"

He looked around. "Just the piano."

"Can't go that far," I said. "Not yet. Who knows, in a couple of months, what might happen? It might disappear some night."

He flashed a grin. "Heaven forbid."

I helped him carry some things out to his van. "So how about a rubber plant for Viola?" I said. "You can see they're beautiful. Bring her by to look at them."

He counted out some bills and handed them over. "Say, Pete, was that true, about the chicken heads?"

"Bad juju true."

"And now they moved?"

"Yes. I'm meeting them next Saturday."

"If he doesn't bump her off first."

That was not outside the realm of possibility. "I don't think he's capable of engineering that kind of action."

Floyd was behind the wheel, idling his engine. He shrugged. "If it happens, I want the piano."

He was a cold one.

"Oh," he said, recalling a nugget, "speaking of pianos, you know what I heard?"

"No idea."

"Katie heard it from her realtor. Walter told me. The insurance people finished combing through the pink house. They found a bunch of money in the piano."

"In the piano?" I echoed.

"Five thousand bucks."

"That's what they turned in," I said.

"Walter said he'd been in there before and looked right into that piano," he said. "He didn't see it. Of course, it was dark."

"No telling how much they really found," I said.

"We're in the wrong business, Pete," he said. The van shifted into reverse like punctuation.

"Aye, aye, Commander," I said, remembering Tonto's famous punch line, "What mean 'we?'"

Voris called that evening, wanting to talk. "I want to come home," she said, before she was disconnected. An hour later, Henry left a message. "You'll have to excuse my wife, Pete. She's very elderly, as you know."

He went on to elaborate still further details of our tacit agreement regarding the radio ad and my fee, something about sharing expenses as well as profits, something else even more demented. He insisted that I was to remain "in constant contact" at all times. I took this last directive with a liberal dose of salt, and resolved to venture out for supplies without further delay.

I made a short list of several items, last but not least of which was a half-pint of Dark Eyes. Why not, eh Willy? I thought. What the hell?

Five thousand bucks. With every step, I berated myself for a lifetime of indecision.

Once a day, at various times, Voris would try to call direct. She'd get a few words in and be disconnected. Then Henry would call and leave a recorded message instructing me either to disregard a previous message or to stand by for further instructions. Day by day he grew more curious as to how the yard sale was progressing, how much money I had made for him and how much I was keeping for myself. I never responded to any messages. When, at last, in a panic, he called me direct, he expressed a fear of being abandoned. All I could do was reassure him that all was well on my end and that I was still looking forward to our meeting on Saturday with great anticipation.

The thought did occur to me that Floyd's suspicion might not fall far short of the mark. If it turned out that Henry was, in fact, a criminal mastermind, and had hatched a sinister plot to dispose of Voris, he would have been remiss not to include a proviso for a foil, such as myself, to provide a distraction while he absconded with whatever plunder he stood to gain.

Although inclined to discount my misgivings, it was less easy to discredit the note of hysteria in Voris' voice each day as her calls to me were aborted.

On the phone to Floyd, I expressed a grave concern over her situation, to which he responded with words to the effect that her fate was already sealed. On this occasion, for some unknown reason, I expected more than a flippant rejoinder from Floyd.

Already, he had stripped the chest and was intent on rebuilding the damaged veneer on the lid with stainable wood dough. He gushed on about the beauty of the wood, trumpeting the artistry of his handiwork, which was indeed noteworthy, but as I hung up it struck me with the clarity of a bellclap that Voris' chest was her property no longer. I had sold her precious possession and would soon be held accountable. Floyd was not about to relinquish his purchase. I was pretty much on my own on this one, me and Mrs. Ferguson.

A few plants and a couple of knickknacks netted about thirty dollars to show for my efforts, with the bulk of the inventory undiminished. When Saturday morning rolled around, I was fairly well-prepared, with Henry's ad punched up, and another one with some improvements. In my eagerness to be on our way forthwith, I met them outside, but Voris had to see for herself what remained of her possessions.

She was devastated by the absence of the chest, gasping and

bawling as she hurried back outside, "You didn't sell my chest? That was my mother's!"

"Chest?" I gave her my best blank look. "Oh. The chest." I winced. "Too late I discovered my error," I said. "An elderly lady was here with her son, what was her name? Ferguson!"

"Pete, you didn't sell my chest." She was taking the loss of it much harder than I expected.

"Sorry, Voris. I mixed up the columns."

She wailed like a lost soul. "Pe-ete!"

"What you get for it?" asked Henry.

"Five bucks."

Voris stopped crying. "I want it back," she said. "That was my mother's chest."

"The lady's name was Mrs. Ferguson."

"What's your total?" said Henry.

"Thirty bucks," I said.

"Which Mrs. Ferguson?" Voris snapped.

"Come on, Pete. Be serious." Henry's voice dropped to a growl.

I handed him a carbuncle of ones. "Voris," I said, "Mrs. Ferguson said she lived on Twelfth Street, I believe. Or Twelfth Avenue."

"Well, you go tell her I want it back, Pete. I mean it."

"Not to worry, Voris."

"I told you not to sell it."

"I'll make every effort to locate her."

"You just tell me where she lives. I'll go see her."

"Voris, believe me, I never would have let it go if I had known it meant so much to you."

"Promise me you'll get it back for me, Pete."

We were all three standing by the car. I turned to Henry and asked him, "Are we going?"

"Get in the car, Irene," he said.

I climbed into the backseat of the station wagon. Voris slid in behind the wheel, still obsessing over the chest. With any luck, Henry'd get her to put a lid on that, but Henry, brooding in the front seat over thirty dollars worth of pilferage, exuded unpredictability.

"Brother," Henry turned around to spread a powerfully ominous grin across the top of the seat, "when we get to the hotel, we're going to have us a little talk."

"Fine." Voris eyed me in the rearview mirror. She turned onto the main road and floored it. Henry turned around and buckled his seatbelt.

"Baby, don't drive so fast," he said.

She drew on her cigarette and laughed as she eased back. She held a girlish posture and looked the two of us over. "A pair of idiots," she said under her breath.

The Hilton was like any Hilton; nice, in a grand way. I walked with the Goodnights to the elevator. Their suite, with a spacious view of I-95, was on the twelfth floor.

Voris clicked on the television. Henry opened the blinds and stepped onto the terrace. He leaned on the rail and motioned to me to join him. "The air is wonderful out here," he said.

The tickle in my throat was acting up. I muffled a cough. "Say, Henry, what about a little something to drink?"

Henry said, "Let's take care of business first."

"The hell you say," rasped Voris, picking up the phone. "I'm calling room service."

Henry beckoned. "Come here, Pete." I joined him on the terrace while Voris ordered gin and vodka and champagne. "I usually drink beer," he said. "I quit drinking liquor."

"Voris," I called, "a coke?"

"But I might have one today."

"Henry," I said, "you've been referring to this meeting we're to have, and here we are at the Hilton. What sort of agenda do you have in mind?"

"Pete, if I was white," he said, "if I was white, I'd own this hotel."

Where was that bellman? "Let's talk about the ad copy."

"First, I want you to meet my friends," he said. He pulled a handgun out from under his jacket, let it rest in the upturned palm of his hand. "Mr. Smith and Mr. Wesson."

"Henry, put it away."

"Just so you to know I'm not fooling, Pete. I'm dangerous."

Voris called when the bellman rang. "Let's have a drink, Henry," I said. "I get the picture."

Of all the corny movie lines, I thought, he would latch on to that one. I still didn't know what he wanted from me. The business angle was a charade. He had to have something else in mind.

We raised an obligatory toast of champagne to our yet unspecified great venture. Three glasses clinked a tenuous bond. I downed mine and poured a glass of something stronger.

"What are you doing for Thanksgiving, Pete?" asked Voris. "You ought to come down. Spend it with us."

"That's a good idea," said Henry.

"Kind of you to invite me," I said, "but transportation is a bit of a problem."

"We'll send you a bus ticket," said Henry. "Round trip. What do you say?"

"That's an idea."

Voris. She lay back on the bed. "This bed is sure soft."

Henry was studying me. "You want my wife?" he asked. "Take her."

Voris purred like a cat, "You take me, ape man."

"Shut up, slave," he said. "You know you want it."

"I'm taking a nap," said Voris. "You men go on about your business. Unless you got something to show me." A dry cackle of mirthless laughter turned to a hacking cough. "Hey, ape man," she choked out a harsh command, "bring me my cigarettes."

Henry tossed her purse onto the bed.

"Afraid I'll bite?" she taunted him.

"Shut up when I tell you, witch," he said. Under his stare, Voris blanched and burrowed deep under the covers. Henry turned back to me. "She's in my power," he said "she done been spellcast."

I poured another drink. "You're some kind of gris-gris, aren't you?"

He beamed at me. "Now you're getting it."

"Fine, Henry. But what is the point, here?"

He put the gun on the table and spun it like a top. I kept my features frozen. The spin slowed and stopped with the barrel pointing at him. He studied me with a secret amusement, his fingertips drumming against themselves. "I was a big man in the rackets once. In Detroit. Had a string of women, dope, everything. My first wife cheated on me and I poisoned her. They never caught me. My second wife died of natural causes. She was scared to death of me."

We stared at each other.

"Am I scaring you, Pete?" he said. "Shocking you?"

"Is that what you're trying to do?"

He reached for the gun and began to fondle it. "How about now?"

My drink wasn't strong enough.

"That one," he jerked his gun hand toward the frail lump under the covers, "she don't scare. She play like she scared, like it's a game. It ain't a game. I got the power. What I tell her to do, that's it." He brandished the gun, pointing it in succession at the bed, at me, and at his own head.

"Would you mind not waving that gun around," I said, overcome with irritation at his pesky bravado.

"Sorry," he said, and put it away.

"Look, Henry, where do I come in? You want to forget about the ad copy, or what?"

"No, hell no," he said. "Let's take a look at it. You're my main man, Pete. We got a business to run. I was just bullshitting, you know."

The precious ad copy came out of the folder at last and we spent a half an hour discussing its merits. The gun never reappeared. I had a couple more drinks. Henry and I passed a slow afternoon imagining immense wealth and fabulous possessions.

When Voris awoke, I pressed her to please drive me home. I wanted to talk to her alone, to warn her about the gun, to find out if it was possible that she was unaware of it. But Henry came along for the ride.

We had agreed that I could remain at the house until the realtor found a suitable tenant. Our business plans would move forward on Henry's end. My hundred dollar fee for the ad copy would be added to my first commission check. Henry had everything under control.

When they dropped me off, Henry got out of the car to unlock the side door for me. Voris reminded me again of my promise to recover her chest from Mrs. Ferguson. Henry saw me inside and shook my hand. "Let me know if you're coming," he said. "I'll mail that ticket."

As soon as their tail lights faded I left the side door unlatched and started walking toward Floyd's. I felt a compelling desire to be around normal people.

Floyd had the chest set up on the porch under lights. He was feathering the patched edges of the veneer on the lid. The chest's transformation was nearly complete. The dark grain glowed with a rich walnut tone through the antique oil finish. The flaws were minuscule where the wood dough patches contrasted with the true stain color.

Viola watched him examine the piece from every angle. "Hi, Pete," she smiled. "You like my chest?"

"It's lovely."

"He's going to give it to me. Aren't you baby?"

Floyd pretended not to hear her.

"Honey," Viola wheedled, "I want it!"

"I kind of wanted to keep it," said Floyd.

"You don't have to give it to me if you don't want to," she said.

Floyd looked at me and rolled his eyes back in his head. "How's Mrs. Ferguson."

"Can't seem to locate her," I said. "She seems to have dropped off the face of the earth."

"You guys are bad," said Viola, going inside.

Floyd made a fire of pine cones and we sat around the fireplace talking of various things. I mentioned the invitation to spend Thanksgiving in Sanford and noted that a counter offer was slow in coming.

"You can eat with us," Viola said, at last, "if you don't want to go down there. You're welcome."

"Thanks very much," I said, "but I should talk to Arthur first. I'd like to spend the day with my boys."

"Call him up," said Floyd.

I'd been putting off the call to Arthur, not wanting to burden him with the news that I was back until I was situated. He had worries enough.

Bradley answered the phone. He said, "Dad. Hey. Glad you called. Listen, don't come over, right? Arthur's having a nervous breakdown over some babe he sent love poems to in Orlando. Come to find out she's a nude dancer at *Club Juana*. He's very depressed. He'll go straight to pieces if he has to deal with you."

"Let me talk to him," I said.

Bradley couldn't keep the impudence out of his voice. "No can do. He's at Mom's. You want the number?"

"Will you be joining him there for Thanksgiving?"

"Probably. Look, Dad, I got company. Call me in a couple of days. Happy Thanksgiving."

The dial tone buzzed in my ear, long after I replaced the phone. Floyd and Viola, no doubt, had their own plans for Thanksgiving. They were nestled on the couch beneath a patchwork afghan, watching a television movie.

I wished them happiness from my heart, and said goodnight. On the walk back to Voris' old place, I reconsidered the invitation to Sanford. Maybe there was a way to cash in the bus ticket.

Chapter Twenty
Ticket to Ride, or Thanks for the Memories

My bus ride to Sanford took three hours, plenty of time to memorialize the carving of many a festive bird at the head of my own table. Thanksgiving Day was not always like this.

A recent phone conversation with Jenny regarding Arthur's malaise was fresh in my mind. The girl in question, to whom Arthur had pledged his heart on a plate, complete with all the trappings of romance; poems, promises, a vision of eternity, had met and married another man who procured for her a position in one of Orlando's finer clubs as an exotic dancer.

Jenny prevailed upon me to refrain from casting any pearls of hard won wisdom Arthur's way. "For now," she emphasized. I had no trouble visualizing the simulated quotation marks she was fond of making with her fingers, an affectation she had long ago adopted solely to annoy me.

There was enough stress in Arthur's life without me adding to it, she said. He had quit his job and taken a number of sleeping tablets, more than enough to counteract a normal case of insomnia. He had then locked the door to his room and slept undisturbed for three days.

Bradley, a former lifeguard with first-aid training at the ready, at length discerned signs of abnormality and broke through the locked door. He seized Arthur's great toe and jerked him bodily from the bed, waking him with a violent drop to the floor. Then he shook Arthur until he cried, and spilled out the sad story of the girl.

The night he quit his job she had called him at work to inform him that she was pregnant. Her husband had left her and she wanted Arthur to be her Lamaze partner.

Arthur never had his younger brother's easy way with girls. Bradley, himself unwounded by love after a procession of conquests, must have been mystified to encounter the depths of Arthur's suffering. No doubt, he found it excessive.

And melodramatic. If Arthur only knew how lucky he was to find out now instead of later what a near miss the dancer was, he might yet come to see that it was all for the best.

"That's the kind of comment," said Jenny, "that is just no help at all."

She, of course, was tactful to a fault. Arthur needed time to reevaluate his feelings, time to think it through on his own. Let him work it out, she said. In other words, without superfluous input from me.

I called Henry after talking to her. The ticket came, as promised. There was no way to cash it in.

So, I would be spending Thanksgiving in Sanford, somewhat preoccupied of mind, but unencumbered by any expectations. The pleasure of my company was requested. To decline their gracious invitation would have disappointed my friends, the Goodnights.

They met my bus at the terminal. Had they been tardy, it might have cost me a quarter, maybe a sojourn on a hard chair. They spared me that, and I was thankful for the consideration, though I might have welcomed a brief delay. For my money, the bus could have gone on and on. Nothing could have prepared me for the sight of them waiting in the arrival zone.

Voris, a tiny old woman, sat beside Henry on a bench, a blue ball cap on her head, bill smartly askew. She wore red heart-shaped sunglasses, and a pink t-shirt with I'M WITH STUPID on the front in big red letters. An extra long cigarette dangled from her ruby lips. She clutched a big black purse in her lap with both hands.

Henry, a giant beside her, wore a stylish, black nylon monogrammed sweatsuit over his red pajama bottoms that sagged below the non-elasticized hem of his trousers. He stared out through mirror shades, his big hands folded at rest on his belly.

They both looked up as the bus wheezed into the bay, scanning the faces at the windows, each of them finding mine within seconds, each of them responding with implausible enthusiasm.

"Pete, we're so glad you could make it," Voris gushed as I stepped down with my bag. She wrapped her arms around me and squeezed.

Henry shook my hand. "Hey, partner."

"How do, folks," I said. They grinned at me like I was the entertainment. Then it dawned on me that I was the entertainment.

"We've got a big day planned," said Voris, as we headed for the car. "First, you have to see the town."

At the stoplight, she pointed out the courthouse and some other buildings. "There it is," she said, "Sanford."

"Nice little town."

"Pete," Voris caught my eye in the rear view mirror, "tell me you found my mother's chest."

She was not going to let me get a meal in me first.

"I can't bear to lose it," she said.

That chest was a pile of rubble and would have remained so without Floyd's attentions. Ownership aside; the important thing was that the chest was restored. Voris's mother would have been proud.

"Voris," I said, "the news on that front is not so good."

"What, Pete, what are you saying?"

For me, it was a moment of truth. If Voris wanted to run all day on that one little battery, she was only going to spoil my appetite.

"Mrs. Ferguson has pancreatic cancer."

"So?" said Voris. "How's my chest going to help her?"

"Well, she was in the hospital last week, having surgery, and her house burned down. She lost everything, including, I'm sorry to say, the chest. Then she moved to Maine."

Voris found my eyes in the mirror again.

"Bid it farewell, Voris."

"Dang you, Pete.

A somber silence ensued. Henry turned to me and said, "How'd you do that?"

"Do what?"

"Shut her up stone cold like that."

"It's cause he's white," Voris snapped at him. "Don't you wish you were white?"

Unruffled by her sarcasm, Henry turned to face me, "If I was white, I'd get over good."

"Think so?" I asked.

"Pete," he said, "If I was you, I'd be successful. Liquor wouldn't be my downfall because I don't drink liquor. You could have been successful, but you drank up all your chances for success. All but one. I'm about to give you one more chance."

"What have I done to deserve it?"

"Nothing, yet," said Henry, "but you got a face. In sales, it all comes down to the image a company projects. Look at Colonel Sanders. Orville Redenbacher. People know their faces and they buy that chicken and popcorn. We're selling stereos, Pete. We need a figurehead."

"Like the cookie guy, Famous Amos?"

"Yeah, only white. If you still had your teeth, I'd put you in a white suit and broadcast your face nationwide. Call you Panama Pete, or something. Can you dance?"

For a set of teeth I could learn to moonwalk.

"Henry, are we talking full dental coverage here? Because, if we're not, what are we talking about?"

"You want some teeth, Pete?" He snapped his fingers. "Nothing to it. Anything can be arranged. Anything. In fact," he paused as if struck by a momentous thought, "I can channel the whole business through you and nobody will even have to know I'm black. We can write off all our expenses." He spoke as if flawless logic had led him to the only reasonable solution. "I'll handle the international end," he went on. "In electronics, the big money's still in Japan."

"Why not have a Japanese figurehead?" I suggested. "Mr. Yamamoto's Dynamic Electronics."

"You think I'm joking? I'm dead serious. We can move on this," he said.

"Honey, I've got news for you," Voris interjected, "you made your move. Look around at where you moved to." She had pulled into an apartment complex. We cruised through a dilapidated housing project. Young turks posturing in small groups shared knowing glances among themselves as the stationwagon passed. "Welcome to our nightmare, Pete," she said. "It doesn't get any better than this."

In her old place, the furniture never called attention to itself. Ample room existed to accommodate a number of matching pieces; hutch, highboy, China cabinet, dining room set, end tables, coffee tables. In the den, a big sofa had sprawled the length of one wall facing a floor-to-ceiling entertainment center against the opposite wall. The new place had no den.

The two bedroom apartment had a combined living and dining room area, two baths, four closets and a small kitchen with an adjoining utility room. The floor plan was universal. I had painted hundreds of them when I was employed. Even empty they were undersized.

No stranger to cramped quarters, I expected to see a crowded apartment crammed to the doors with her furniture. Until she opened the door, I had full confidence in my ability to visualize a crowded room. I had presumed that there were limits involved, which reasonable people did not exceed. As the door opened, I was jolted by the folly of that presumption.

In the front room, the dark wood furniture was arranged in tight compression against the available walls. The monolithic highboy and the china cabinet loomed large on either side of the entrance, casting long shadows. Boxes stacked in columns reached almost to the ceiling. The big sofa bisected the room and faced an entertainment center much reduced in size. Part of it appeared to have been sawed off to fit in through the narrow entry.

The room was divided, not in half, but between the outer and the inner room. The outer room, along the walls, was decorated to Voris' taste with doilies on the tables and dainty crystal lamps illuminating artifacts from her earlier life; framed photographs of her ancestors, and tiny porcelain treasures. She collected elephants. An array of elephant figurines in every color and size adorned the shelves and table surfaces. The center of the room contained the sofa, the columns of unpacked boxes containing Henry's stereo and computer equipment, and, wedged between two columns, the television console.

They had found a place for the dining room table and chairs between the kitchen and the utility room area. Voris stepped through the maze, turning sideways, twisting and squeezing through the narrow passage. I followed the ludicrous spectacle of Henry following her trail, twisting and squeezing through the same narrow passage. "Like living in a china shop with a bull," said Voris, as I emerged from the labyrinth and joined them in the kitchen, "or a bullshitter, one."

Henry obliged her with a good-natured chuckle and opened the oven door to inspect the turkey. "About done," he announced.

"I'll say when it's done," said Voris. She took a peek at the bird and slammed the door shut. "Not yet. Pete, would you like something to drink?"

"Splendid idea."

"Why don't you show him the study, Henry? I'll bring your drinks," she said. "You want a beer?"

He consulted his watch before answering. It was not quite eleven. "I'll have tea," he said.

"Hot or cold?"

"Whatever's easier for you, hon,"

"Beer is easier," she retorted.

"Ok, a beer, then."

"My lord and master," her sarcasm echoed down the hall.

Henry tapped his temple with a finger. "She's losing it up here," he confided. "Won't be long now."

The study was to be his new computer room. Boxes of

unassembled components were stacked against the walls. Gratified to find an extra chair in the room, I took it. Gone the days of crouching on a footstool.

"Time is on our side," he said.

Voris brought our beverages in tall glasses and withdrew, silent as a geisha. Henry tasted his beer and set the glass aside. "Warm!" He scowled. "Bitch ought to be shot. Pow. Goodnight, Irene." He tried another sip and sighed. "Don't have the heart for wet work anymore. If she'd kick off on her own, it'd be different. But she won't." He took a larger swallow. "She's going to live forever."

All I could think about was Arthur, saddled with another man's child by a scheming and unworthy woman. Henry's spurious confidences struck me as a lot of rodomontade. He did have the gun, though, and I supposed, it was something of a trial for him to resist the urge to show it to me again.

Aside from a meal to which a number of strings were attached, I had nothing to gain by being there, although, to the promise of teeth, I was particularly vulnerable. Were it not for my boy scout training, for a set of teeth I might have consented to hold her still while he reloaded. Lucky for Voris, I was a good scout, bound by a solemn oath to remain steadfast, loyal and true.

"How much do you need," Henry asked with casual interest, "to get your movie project off the ground?"

"About five mil," I said. "Why? You interested?"

He gave me a long searching look. "Like I said before, anything's possible."

"Henry," I said, "You want to talk venture capital? Super. I'll give you a number in Vegas to call. Only let's not joke about the movie business. I'm not in the mood."

"No offense," said Henry. "I was just wondering."

"None taken."

I sipped my drink and waited for the next shoe to drop. Unless I missed my guess, he would find a way back to the teeth angle.

A silence spread in which the rattling of ice in my empty glass was the only sound. I looked around at the boxes neatly stacked in piles. The reassembly of the computer had yet to begin. "I'd have thought you'd have had it together by now," I said.

He gave an oddly disinterested shrug. "I need to install another outlet. Should have two more. If I run it off one, might start a fire. The whole building could go up."

"That would be messy," I said.

"Risky, too," he said. "We can't go that route."

"Certainly not," I concurred. That was as close as I ever came to collusion.

He stood up and with ponderous solemnity held out a nearly empty bottle of beer. "Partner," he said, "let's have a toast."

My glass was empty. I held it up and he clinked it. "Gee, Henry," I said, "What are we toasting? Mightn't I have a Thanksgiving refill?"

"Of course," he said, masking vexation with a chuckle. "Beer should be cold by now. Let's see how the bird's coming along." He stood holding the door open for me, a tight grin on his face. As I stepped past him into the hall, he whispered, "Be better with some teeth, wouldn't it?"

Voris had the table set with her good China. A colorful linen tablecloth with a handstitched pilgrim motif was perfectly centered, the corner creases falling in natural, effortless lines. Most pleasing to the eye were the silver platters and the silver gravy boats polished and sparkling with the sheen of rare usage.

"Voris, you've outdone yourself," I said. "This is superb."

A gauntlet of side dishes were arranged in oval symmetry around the centerpiece, the festive bird, done to a turn on a silver platter. The initial carving, it was impossible not to notice, had been done beforehand. Neatly sliced slabs of white meat were fanned like playing cards on a serving plate.

"Dig in," said Voris, as we took our seats.

Henry, at the head of the table, bridled at finding the traditional privilege of his chair pre-empted by his spouse. "I was going to carve the bird," he said.

"Oh, for heaven's sake," Voris snapped, "don't be so peevish."

"Extraordinary stuffing, Voris," I said.

"Thank you, Pete. Did you say something, Henry?" she asked.

With a violent stab of his fork, he speared two thick slabs of turkey and transferred them to his plate. It struck me that she was better off not knowing what Henry might have mumbled. His eyes bored into hers with a menacing intensity, but she shrank not, nor did she look away. "Well?" she defied him, "what the hell are you looking at?"

"The hell you think?" Henry shot back. "A man can't even carve his own turkey?"

"Oh, your turkey? You bought it, did you? You cooked it? Well, have at it, pilgrim. There's a whole other side to carve."

"These glazed peas are wonderful," I said.

"I got your pilgrim," Henry muttered.

"Do you now?" Voris fluttered, warming to the game. "Why, wherever has he been?"

I passed the bowl of peas to Henry. He stopped glowering long enough to spoon a portion onto his plate, and passed it back to me without speaking. I followed with other dishes, potatoes, carrots, corn, stuffing, until his plate was full and he had begun in earnest to sample Voris' cooking.

"This is good, baby," he said, attempting, at least, to sound conciliatory. "I might keep you after all."

"Thank you, hon," said Voris. "Glad you like it."

"Fabulous dinner," I said, "stupendous."

"I'm so thankful you're here to share it with us, Pete. Neither of us has any family living, you know, and we're both thankful to have you for a friend."

"The pleasure's all mine," I said.

"My old friends don't call me anymore," she said. "You're the only friend either one of us have. Sometimes the loneliness gets to me. Henry, he won't even go outside without me. He won't even take out the garbage. I have to carry it out to the dumpster. All those young bucks out there, they look at me and touch themselves when I go by."

"How you talk," said Henry. "Young bucks touching themselves. I won't have that. I'll shoot your ass."

The gun was on the table, next to his plate, the barrel pointing at the cavity filled with stuffing.

"Henry," said Voris, "what are you going to do with that gun?"

"When I finish eating this fine dinner," he said, "I might blow your head off."

Voris looked to me for some kind of sign. With a nod, I tried to emit tranquility. "Henry," I said, "is this necessary?"

"Just eat your dinner, partner. I got it covered."

"Henry, think about it," I said. "A thing like this could be very bad for business."

"You heard the bitch. She's out there trolling for young meat. She can't be satisfied."

"They do look at me," said Voris. "They want me. I can feel it when I walk past them. They all want me."

"I'll kill your ass dead," said Henry, picking up the gun and brandishing it.

Voris laughed, taunting him. "You think you scare me? Hah! What have I got to live for? Go ahead and shoot. See if I care."

"Say your prayers, Irene," said Henry, aiming the gun at her head. He cocked the trigger.

Voris stared at Henry, daring him to shoot. Then she wavered, looked away, and began to tremble.

I pushed my chair back from the table and stood. "That's enough, Henry," I said, moving toward him. He swung the gun over to me and pointed it at my stomach.

"You taking her side, Pete? I thought we were partners."

His grin was more smug than wicked. Voris was sobbing, her face in her hands. If he would really shoot, I had no way of knowing. I stood calmly awaiting an opening.

"You want her for yourself, don't you?" He shook his head in mock confusion. "White folks always stick together. I done spent her money." His galling laugh sought only to rile me. "Might be enough left in the kitty for some teeth," he gloated.

Since deciding to intervene, I had discounted the verbal option, deeming it an inadequate response to the situation. Action was required, to remove or neutralize the weapon, and, if at all possible, to restore the former spirit of holiday cheer.

"Henry, this is all a misunderstanding," I said.

"Sit down, Pete," he said, "you ain't going to do nothing."

"I think I'd like a drink," I said.

Voris slid her chair back, saying, "I'll get it."

Henry swung the gun to this right to cover her. I followed the arc of his arm with my body, falling with my reaching weight across the edge of the table in a well-placed lunge for his wrist. His chair spun off balance from my momentum and we toppled together into a corner.

I slammed his wrist on the baseboard as we hit the floor, heard the hammer click without firing. Henry went limp beneath me. A pitiful sob whined in his throat as I rolled off him. Voris had picked up the gun. "It's not loaded," she said. "That son of a bitch."

"I'm fine, Voris," I said, getting slowly to my feet. "Thanks so much for asking."

"Sorry, Pete. You all right?"

Dusting myself off, I nodded. "The gun was empty?"

She handed it to me. "Where can I put it?" I asked, and she snatched it back.

"I'll hide it," she said, disappearing into their bedroom.

Henry pulled himself up and sat on the floor with his head bowed, wringing his hands in a farcical display of penitence. He kept his downcast eyes averted, and gave the appearance of silent prayer.

"I had to stop you, Henry," I said. "You left me no choice."

"You did right," he said. "You did."

"It's all right, hon," said Voris. Having hidden the gun, she offered him a warm embrace.

"I'll have that drink now," I said, "if I may."

"Help yourself," said Voris.

In the kitchen, I checked the time. It was only one-thirty. I fixed a stout drink, took it into the living room, switched on the television with the remote, sank into the sofa and began to flip channels.

I remembered how Clarence used to annoy me with that habit of flipping to a new channel every fifth of a second. I missed the old guy. In my imagination, he was watching me now, shaking his head in disappointment, saying, "What did I tell you?"

Voris called out to me, "Pete, I think you hurt him. His eyes don't look right. What if he has a concussion?"

Christ, I thought, two more hours.

"Help me get him down the hall to the bedroom," she said. "I'm calling the doctor."

"The couch," Henry groaned.

"Let's put him on the couch," Voris amended.

"He can walk."

"Well, damn, you knocked him senseless," she said, "help me get him up."

After two hernia operations, I did not relish the thought of a third.

"Wait a minute, then. Let's see if this works."

Henry's blank expression indicated an absence of consciousness. Standing in front of him, I leaned over, held up my middle finger in front of his face and asked him, "how many fingers do you see, Henry?"

He recoiled, not actor enough to feign indifference to insult. "He'll be fine," I said, when he failed to answer.

He dropped the facade and managed a sheepish, ingenuous smile.

"Oh, Henry," Voris threw her arms around him again.

"You got me that time, Pete," he said, at once his amiable old self again.

Voris rocked him in her arms. "Oh, Henry, you gave us a scare, you did. Are you sure you're all right? Do you want anything?"

"I'm kind of hungry for a turkey sandwich," he said.

"You want one, too, Pete?" Voris asked.

"If you make it to go," I said.

"There's a ball game on," said Henry.

"I can't miss my bus," I said.

"Hell, you won't," said Henry. He found the remote between the cushions of the couch and located a football game. "That's more like it," he said, dropping his weight lengthwise. "Honey," he called, "I'll take a beer, too."

And so normality of a sort returned to the Goodnight household, thanks to me. Although I received no thanks for my peacemaking role, I did have several cold turkey sandwiches stuffed deep in my coat pockets as I boarded the return bus. Nothing between them had changed. The day was merely over.

After an hour or so of football and vacuous commentary, I had a moment alone with Voris in the kitchen. When I asked if she felt safe with Henry, she made light of my concern. "It wasn't even loaded," she said.

"This time," I said. "What about next time?"

"You don't know my Henry," she smiled. "He wouldn't hurt me." She patted me on the cheek, a mincing, ingenue touch. "The very idea," she fluttered.

Another man might have called it a day about then, let the ancient, instinctive obligation go unheeded. I couldn't. "Voris," I said, "listen to me. Is this what you want? To live in a dollhouse with a mental patient running your financial affairs? After today's incident, you should consider reassuming your own power of attorney. At the very least, consult a lawyer. For your own good. Before everything's gone."

"Everything's already gone," she said, "except the house. We're selling it next. That Henry," she shook her head in fond exasperation. "He's the devil."

On that note, I conceded defeat and began to keep an ever more watchful eye on the clock. I went through the motions of watching the game with Henry, sinking into the sofa beside him, but my thoughts retreated from the present into a misty reverie of my happy boyhood and youth, days when my future shown bright as a new dime. Captain of the debating team, President of my Senior

Class, voted Most Likely to Succeed. How did such a promising young paragon as I come to fall so short of my noble goals? I asked myself that question once again. No single answer ever sprang to mind. On the success side of the ledger, I had only my boys to weigh against a rather lengthy string of setbacks. I hoped they were having a pleasant Thanksgiving with their mother.

On the way to the station the Goodnights and I exchanged our various pleasantries. I had a key to their house and an agenda. My sales territory extended throughout the Western Hemisphere. They dropped me off by the station door, with a hearty handshake and a farewell kiss. "Remember what I said," I told Voris.

"Thanks for coming, Pete," she said.

As they drove away, I felt in my pocket for the return ticket, my most valuable possession. It was there, my ticket from nowhere to nowhere. I gave thanks. Thanks for the memories.

Chapter Twenty-One
The Rubes-Live, or Let There Be Drums

The more things changed, the more they remained the same. Wiser men than I had made that observation. I was walking along in a philosophical mood down a side street one morning, on my way to the office supply store to buy a new typewriter ribbon. I also had some Christmas cards in my coat pocket to mail, including one for Floyd, when he pulled up beside me in his van, as he often did when he saw me out walking. Wordlessly, I opened the door and got in. As the van chugged on down the street, I asked him, "Miss the cab business much?"

"Don't laugh," he said, "if things don't pick up soon, I may have to go back to the cab."

"Sounds like a country western song."

"Not a happy tune," he said. "My business is going down the tubes. I'm fixing to pack it in and go to work for somebody else."

I pretended to strum a hillbilly guitar and drawled, "Fixing to pack it in ... go to work for somebody else."

"Paying rent with credit cards. It's killing me to keep that place. I'm going to have to give it up, I know, but the day I move in with Viola Henley, Pete, I'm done for."

"Is that your plan?"

"That's Plan B," he said. "But the longer I hold out, the more I get the feeling my days are numbered."

Boy, did I know that feeling.

"Anyway, Merry Christmas. This'll be the last Christmas I spend in that house, so don't feel like a stranger, Pete. You know you're welcome."

I handed him his Christmas card. "I was going to mail this, but since the address may soon be incorrect, perhaps I'd better hand deliver it."

"Thanks, Pete," he said. "As ever, how very thoughtful." He glanced at the card signed, "As Ever, Pete," and turned up another side street. "By the way, where are you headed?"

He altered his course toward my destination, moving unhurriedly through the neighborhood grid of avenues and streets with stop signs at every corner, which he acknowledged either by slowing down or turning right.

"Stop by later," he said, "We've got a couple of new tunes."

"What's the name of the band this week?" I asked.

"Walter likes The Rhythm Squires," he said, with a flicker of jocularity. "Your basic toss up between that and The Rubes. What do you think?"

"Rubes," I said, casting my vote.

He dropped me at the doorstep of the office supply store and offered to wait if I made my purchases quickly. Such largesse was seasonal, the Yuletide softening of his flinty heart.

"I'll be brief," I said, hitching my step like a spry Walter Brennan in a hurry, ever mindful of the value of a ride. I preferred not to rush when I shopped though I had no love of walking, either. List in hand; ribbon, envelopes, White-out, I was in and out in ten minutes.

"Meter's running," he said, as I climbed back in.

"Now," I said, "if you could take me by the liquor store and then to Voris', I'd appreciate it."

He turned down another side street. "How went Thanksgiving? Pretty smooth?"

"You wouldn't believe it," I said.

"She still hot about her chest?"

"Taken care of," I said.

"No dangling obligations?"

"I told you I'd handle it."

"So you did, Pete. So you did."

We drove through the drive through and picked up a pint. "What about the piano, Pete?" he asked, when we were rolling again. "What if you sold it to Mrs. Ferguson for, say, two hundred bucks?"

"Let me think about it," I said. "That whole situation is unstable at best right now."

"It's not like I want to rob her," he said.

"Of course not."

"I want to pay her for it. I just don't want to have to pay her very much. By the way, can you make it today? I know you've got more important things to do and all, but we need your beat."

"Scale for drummers still twenty an hour?"

"Around four." He pretended not to hear. "Let there be drums."

"Let there be paintbrushes," I said, "and typewriter cases. And pots and pans."

"The beat goes on," he laughed, "ladadadadee."

A short while later, at Voris' house, I took a closer look at her piano and examined my conscience. There was a line I chose not to cross, demarcated by the piano. Not for nothing was I blessed with innate integrity. Now it loomed on the higher ground, above the moral vacuum of rationale. I could not be party to any more larcenous transactions on behalf of Mrs. Ferguson, may she rest in Maine, not without risking its forfeiture. This I would not do.

Not, at any rate, without significant recompense. Not like last time.

Aside from the piano, and the tools in the garage, the house was vacant. The new tenants were due to move in any day. All was in readiness, and, of course, my own instructions were to move within the week.

The letters I was writing had to do with a plan I was formulating to return to New York. My stepdad, not in the best of health at eighty-five, was living alone in the family manse on Staten Island. In storage, in the vaulted attic of the manor home where I grew up, was a priceless antique grandfather clock that my mother had willed to me eleven years earlier, along with various trunks and boxes filled with family heirlooms that would languish in probate indefinitely should Jack, my dear stepdad, pass away before I claimed my inheritance.

The last of the Foster family treasures were in that attic. For my boys' sake, I had to get up to the estate and settle the business. My fondest hope was that Arthur and I might both somehow manage to be with Jack for New Year's Eve. I continued to hope for what amounted to a miracle and meanwhile wrote desperate letters to distant friends appealing to their generous natures.

I had made no concrete plans to move, though it looked like events were once again leading me back to a Christmas at the Deadbeat Hotel. It wasn't New York, but then, perhaps timing was, in fact, everything. The clock was still there, in a safe place.

I dropped a note to Rico and Marilyn to thank them for the card they sent, a cheery greeting from Las Vegas with a fifty tidily tucked inside.

Rico was a never-say-die kind of guy. A class act all the way. He kept pitching the script, his eye on the prize. "It can happen, Pete," he said to me time and again. "It happens every day. Times change, but you've got a piece of work, pal. They'll come around."

He would have been great as the itinerant jazzman, Billy Highpockets, the role I'd written for him in the script. Oscar material, Best Supporting Actor. "Thanks, Rico," I wrote, with tears in my eyes for having put the touch on him of all people at Christmas.

My envelopes were addressed and sealed when Voris called. I was nearly out the door, intending not to answer, but then I heard her cracked voice leaving a message, and I knew something was wrong.

"Pete," she spoke in a hoarse monotone, "Can you come down?"

"I'm here, Voris," I said, picking up.

"He found the gun, Pete. They came and got him."

"Voris, what happened? He found the gun and what?"

"He made me beg for my life. Beg for my life. That's what he likes. He didn't shoot me, though. He went outside to fire. Then he came in and called 911. They got him now. He's back in the nuthouse."

"You're sure you're alright, Voris?" I asked.

"I'm a little shook up, Pete. Can you come down?"

"Voris," I said, "I'm tied up here at the moment."

"Ok, then," she said, in a fading voice.

"Voris, maybe now you'll talk to your lawyer?"

"I guess," she said. "Henry called this morning. He asked who was I sleeping with. Can you believe him?"

"Voris, call your lawyer," I said. "Posthaste."

"Maybe I will, Pete. You take care now. Happy New Year."

"Happy New Year, Voris."

I gathered up the letters that were ready to mail and set out for the mailbox. Walking helped me think sometimes. Would Voris move back now? I wondered. Either way, my tenure was up at her place. I dropped the letters in the box and headed for Floyd's.

The Rhythm Squires. The name suggested Edwardian costumes, ruffled shirts with droopy sleeves. Out of the question. The Mournful Harmony Twins, was an apter, earlier name I had liked. The Rubes gave less away, though. I could picture it on a marquee.

They were in fine fettle. Walter had checked off work at three and hadn't had more than two drinks, tops. He was strumming and Floyd was tapping the wooden xylophone as their voices intertwined in twinlike mournful harmony.

They were doing one of Walter's songs. I listened for a moment with my hand on the doorknob, to the lagging rhythm, the flat, atonal harmony behind the mordant verse:

I'm gonna find myself a woman
Tie her to a chair
I'll come home from work on time
And she'll be sitting there

They were stalking the hit parade, no question. But boy, could they use a drummer.

Stepping through the tangle of microphone wires into the makeshift studio, I took my place next to Walter on the long blue couch. The typewriter case was set up on the coffee table, with a towel underneath it to muffle the sound, and my two china bristle brushes on the side. I gave the brushes a familiar twirl, rolling my wrists through a few preliminary flourishes, I could never get used to not having a cymbal, but for scale I could use a spaghetti pot.

"Let there be drums," I said.

"Testing, testing," Walter crooned into his microphone, in a suave parody of an amateur night host, "Good evening, Ladies and Gentlemen." He had a natural voice, silky smooth and resonant. "And now here's something I hope you might really enjoy."

Floyd set the recording levels and waited for a signal from Walter.

"From Westchester, Connecticut," Walter strummed a bland accompaniment, "let's have a big hand for our next contestants."

"Sir Walter and the Rhythm Squires," Floyd announced.

"Sir Walter," Walt repeated, "Sir Walter and the Raleighs."

"C'mon, Walt," I said, the pro in me picking up the underlying beat and we fell into step like a couple of mules dragging a creaking covered wagon down a dusty bumpy road. Any minute Gene Autrey might ride up alongside singing about the tumbling tumbleweeds.

"Yipiteyeyeyo," said Floyd, picking up his maracas. "Get along little dogie, 'tis your misfortune and none of my own."

"All right, let's do it," said Walter, suddenly all business. "What song are we doing?"

"Uncle Willard's Chili," said Floyd, tossing Walt a curve.

"Hit it," said Walt. The tape was rolling on another Rube classic. The future was a bright pearl, waiting to be plucked. Historians would do well to note that the seeds of The Rubes' phenomenal success were sown during these archival sessions, under adverse conditions against impossible odds, which they overcame, as history and their platinum legend has shown.

When the tape was played back, we were always astonished that it sounded no worse than it did. There were moments of spontaneous chemistry. Some songs would go in one take and by common consent were considered definitive versions. Other songs took several takes and required a bit more rehearsal. If one song hit a snag, we would move on to another. Floyd had a file folder full of songs, and Walter had a few of his own.

We were practicing Walt's song when the phone rang. Lyle Stone was calling from the local bar to invite the band to their first live gig. "We're not ready," said Floyd. Then he gave the phone to Walter. "He wants to talk to you."

"Yeah, man," said Walter. "We can handle it. How many minutes? Ok." He hung up and said, "We got a gig!"

"Oh, no," said Floyd. "Walter, how drunk are you?"

"Hey," said Walter, "we can do this. We're as ready as we'll ever be."

I waited for someone to explain to me what was happening.

"There's a guy playing guitar by himself on the deck," said Floyd. "Lyle said he'll let us go on when he takes a break."

"No drumset?" I asked.

"I don't guess you want to haul your typewriter case and paintbrushes up there," said Floyd.

"Not particularly, no."

"Let's just go up there," said Walter.

"You guys go," I said.

"No, come on, Pete," said Walt. "I'll buy you a drink. We'll all go up there. Right, Floyd? We'll all go up there."

Floyd was unplugging microphone wires and putting the living room back in order. "Yeah, come with us, Pete," said Floyd. "We might need moral support."

"All right," I said. "We should be going, then," I indicated Walter, with a nod to Floyd, "before, you know."

"Don't worry," said Walter. His hands were shaking as he tried to coax a last spark out of his lighter. "I'm a professional," he said, puffing a smoke cloud.

The phone rang twice more before we left. Viola called and Floyd arranged to meet her at the bar. Then Lyle called back to make sure we were coming. We climbed into Floyd's van and headed up to Mango's Beach Bar.

The journey was silent and tremulous. "I'm a professional," Walter said. "I've been on stage hundreds of times, thousands of times."

"Not lately, though, right?" said Floyd.

"I know what to do. You're not getting stagefright, are you, bud?"

"Just don't forget what song we're doing."

"I'm a professional," said Walter.

"You want to do your song first? That's fine."

"Yes," said Walt, "then what?"

"I don't know, we'll see what happens."

There weren't many people on the deck, maybe twelve. Though the weather was warm, it wasn't quite summer, and most of the Christmas revelers were inside the bar. Lyle introduced the guitar player, who was more than willing to take a break. I took a seat at a table a little ways back from the front row, leaving the key players to hash out their plan.

Floyd brought me a drink. "They never heard of this drink before," he said. "Vodka and coke, what kind of drink is that?"

"Thanks, kid," I said. Too bad there wasn't a drumset. I would have enjoyed putting some crisp, jazzy touches behind their debut. Instead, I was a spectator, waiting to witness the great event.

My mind wandered backward some thirty years, to a night in Miami, a night I liked to think of as the night of the white drummer. I was driving homeward after a late engagement, a formal affair in honor of a producer friend of mind, who was celebrating his latest coup, a series of propaganda broadcasts for the Cuba Libre Foundation. I kept hearing a saxophone playing sweet and plaintive. I drove around the block, trying to locate the source, and finally parked the car and traced the haunting music to a single door. I was twenty-eight or twenty-nine, a hundred eighty pounds, too confident to be scared. The door was unlocked so I went in.

In darkness, the soulful music was playing: a five man combo, drums, organ, guitar, sax and trumpet. An all black band, an all black audience, an all black bar, and there I was, a white drummer, drawn like an iron filing to the magnetic music.

Nobody bothered me. The music was very cool. When the band took a break, I asked him if I might sit in for him on the next set. A couple of numbers. He could take a little longer break.

He said, "Sure, man."

In those days, if it was jazz, I knew the tune. The bank looked at me in my white dinner jacket with raised eyebrows. I had just come from the party. I looked good. They kicked it off and I fell right in the pocket with them. A couple of minutes later, they were all smiling at the white drummer. After the set, the drummer came up and complimented me, "Man, you sound black," he said.

During breaks, they switched on the jukebox. I was so carried away with the pure enjoyment of drumming I didn't want to stop. I kept time very softly with the brushes, practicing subtle patterns, unaware that I was violating a house rule.

A large man came over to me and gently put his hand on my arm.

"Don't play," he said, "while the pooky-poo is playing."

"Man," I said, "I'm just doing some fills."

His voice grew suddenly deeper. "Don't play while the pooky-poo is playing," he repeated.

"The pooky-poo?"

He pointed to the jukebox. "The pooky-poo."

I looked around and the room didn't look quite so friendly anymore. I put down the brushes and sauntered over to the bar. I had a drink and let things settle back to normal before I made my exit. Thus ended the night of the white drummer.

Jenny used to love jazz, one of our many common interests. Sunday afternoons at the MaiKai, local jazz players had a regular thing going, different guests would fall by. The Tad Todd Trio, Zack Bookout. I knew them well, played with all of them, until they closed the MaiKai. Jenny wept for my sake when that happened. She knew what drumming had come to mean to me. It was my creative outlet, my link with the music I loved. There was to be no drum playing for me after that bar closed, not for a very long time, and then, not on real drums.

Viola joined me at the table. "Isn't this exciting?" she said.

"History in the making," I said.

Lyle Stone was going to sing with them. He was a Rube from way back, though not a Mournful Harmony Twin. He had also written a song with which they were all familiar. The format was to do three songs, one of each of theirs. Walter was impatient to begin.

While he was tuning his guitar, several members of the audience departed, leaving a crowd of seven people on the deck, nine, including Viola and myself.

"We better get started before the rest of them leave," said Floyd.

"Ok, hit it," said Walt. They were off and running.

When gauging the effect of unfamiliar material on an audience, first impressions are often misleading. In the no man's land between indifference and polite approval lies an infinite sea of mixed reactions.

Improbably, The Rubes had stage presence. Walter's voice was charismatic and he even remembered the words. I felt like cheering the lads myself when I heard a female fan squeal in adoring delight. Viola, doing her part like a carnival shill, left nothing to chance. Next, they would all light matches, I thought. Walter beamed like an enraptured angel, mesmerized by the incredible sound of applause.

"That went very well," I said to Viola. "Did it cost you much to fix the house?"

She laughed. "Not very."

The next two numbers also went well, but they were wise not to try a fourth. Lyle drew a blank on the second song, forgetting his last verse. Floyd backed him up and they got through that one. Then Floyd sang his song, without hesitation, stagefright, or an ear for tonality. He bluffed on, uncannily synchronized with Walter straight through to the end, with Lyle's droning harmonics adding a rubrical dimension off to the side.

When the song was over, it was good to be among friends. Drinks all around and many pats on backs.

"To the tippety," Floyd kept saying to his bandmates, "to the tiptop of the tippety top. Aye, lads, where are we going?"

Walter stared at him like he was crazy.

"To the tippety top," said Floyd, murdering a Liverpool accent.

We didn't linger. Lyle stayed. Walt and I rode home with Floyd. "It was a magic night," said Walter. All things were possible on such a night. "We wowed 'em, bud," said Walter, getting out. "Kate's home. She'll probably go to bingo. If she does I might come back over."

"Not tonight, Walt," said Floyd. "I've had enough."

"Ok, boys." Walt said goodnight and went inside.

Walter walked across the yard with his guitar case in hand. "There goes a professional," said Floyd.

"He came through for you."

We were sitting in the van outside the house, appreciating the starlit sky and the night's quiet stillness. From the next street over, a faint echo of Christmas carolers drifted through the silence.

"Your room's just like you left it, Pete," said Floyd, at last. "Merry Christmas."

"Thanks, Dad," I said. "When are you moving?"

"Did I say I was moving?"

"Why fight it, kid," I said. "You two have a good thing going."

Floyd did not appear to be ecstatic over the prospect. "I told her I'd do it, move in with her. This time next month I'll be shutting it down. Have to sell a bunch of junk and stuff, put the rest in storage. Paint the place up a little, get my deposit back. What am I going to do with all the crap in the garage?"

"Have a yard sale."

"Old paint cans, ten cents a gallon."

"I can help."

"Well, you've got a month here. After that, I'm out of the picture. And, of course, I won't be taking you with me."

"How far away does Viola live?" I asked.

"Not within your usual walking distance. But it's not just that,

Pete. It won't be the same. You won't be able to hang out for great periods of time. You know that, don't you?"

"Say no more," I said. With any luck, I'll be in New York by then, anyway."

"That would be nice," said Floyd. "And oh, so reasonable. You only need, what, about a thousand dollars?"

"Something like that," I said. He knew about the clock from previous years. It was hardly a new idea of mine to go back to New York. Every year, I must have voiced the same impossible dream.

"Man, just get a bus ticket and go," he said. "When you get up there, sell the damn clock and you'll have some money. I can't believe how much time you've wasted thinking about something so simple."

"You don't understand," I said. "The clock's been in my family for generations. My boys should have it."

"You don't think they'll sell it? Man, wake up, Pete. Year after year, you keep piddling around, and that clock's still sitting there. Let's be sentimental. Let's not ever sell it. Never mind being poverty-stricken, let's hand it down to future generations."

Ah, youth, I thought, to be so decisive, so free of doubt.

The old house was chilly inside. He cut the heat on and went around shutting all the windows.

"Viola's coming over," he said. "She says this place is always cold."

"She should have been here last year," I said, "when the pipes froze."

Chapter Twenty-Two
Decline and Fall of the Deadbeat Hotel,
or Calling All Rubes

My last instructions from Voris were to turn my key over to the realtor. She had decided to stay on in Sanford while Henry was ill, which was a lot like saying she might never return.

I had some last minute details to attend to at her place before the new tenants arrived. The gleaning of her refrigerator had yielded a selection of condiments I bagged to bring to Floyd's and then left on her kitchen counter. The bag's foremost treasure was a large bottle of tabasco sauce, half-full, easily a five year supply. Floyd would appreciate it, despite the mature appearance of the rusty brown liquid.

Many times in our long association he had shared with me the staple of his diet, macaroni and cheese, seasoned to perfection with pepper, onions and hot sauce. Invariably a tasty blend. To my compliments, his uniform response was, "Yeah, I sure can cook!"

Incumbent upon me as his perennial tenant, yardman, dishwasher and friend, was the straight man's duty to endure without redress his vituperative stabs at levity, such as his occasional habit of introducing me as his "live-in gnome," an appellation no less depreciative for being inaccurate. At six feet, I far exceeded the height specifications of a gnome.

He was referring, of course, to my customary perch on a barstool at the kitchen counter, where, with my typewriter, I occupied the barest minimum of space.

I had already moved most of my things out of Voris' house. The bag of condiments was my main reason for returning. That and a last once over. Floyd volunteered to drive me over and back. He wanted another look at the piano.

"So, how do we move it?" He asked as if I, being a furniture mover, would know.

"No idea," I said. "With pulleys?"

"Some kind of rolling ramp, maybe," he went on, considering the logistics, "we can probably rent one. Wonder what they're called?"

"A piano mover?" I ventured.

"Could be," he conceded. "Did you mention to Voris about maybe selling it."

"Timing in this sort of situation," I said, "is everything. You understand."

"You're saying it's not a good time?" he asked. "When might be a better time?"

"She can be lucid one minute and hysterical the next. You don't want hysteria," I said.

"I want a piano," he said.

"Why? You can't play."

"Say what you will," he said, fibrillating his outstretched fingers, "call me a foppish ne'er do well, but these hands cry out for melody."

Floyd kept flexing his fingers and looking at his hands, bracing them above the keys. "Play, magic fingers," he murmured, and lightly rippled a quivering glissando.

"Maestro," I said.

I had the bag of condiments in hand, all I was likely to get out of the Goodnight affair, aside from my worldwide sales territory. I locked the side door and left the key under the mat.

The sun was setting on the Deadbeat Hotel. An aura of time suspended hung about the place. To me, the old house was emblematic of the friendship that existed between Floyd and myself.

Brothers under the skin, he was like another son to me, yet, in a way, he reminded me of my father, the Commander.

In no respect did he resemble my father, a dashing naval officer, stern and imperious of bearing, accustomed to blind loyalty and unquestioning obedience. Still, I often found myself crisply saluting Floyd and placating him with an "Aye, aye, Commander," the way I used to placate my father when he was bilious.

Floyd, as a rule, cast a cold eye on sentiment. I knew not to natter on to him about the inexpressible sorrow one sometimes is pierced with when the realization that a dear friend is moving hits home. For me to react with less than my usual aplomb would not have been seemly, but the truth was that I was rattled by the aftershock of his decision to move.

My own feelings of loss were of secondary, even tertiary import. The concerns of lovers must always come first, else what is the law? Though I sensed trepidation in Floyd, I resolved early on to venture forth no word of counsel in the matter. Regardless of residences that come and go, or women, of whom the same is often said, I remained, as ever, a friend with his best interests at heart. I understood that it was time for him to move on and sincerely wished him only the best in all his pursuits and endeavors.

I always said the kid had talent. As a songwriter, he was in the wrong town. To mail cassettes off to Nashville was one thing, to go there was quite another.

Not that I had any room to talk. My own life was riddled with red-letter days and wrong decisions. Hindsight qualified me as a walking example of talent misapplied. That I could have done this or that was no longer the point. The point, the only point, was never to lose sight of the goal, which, to hear Floyd talk, was Nashville. He owed himself a shot at the town if he really wanted to hear his songs on the radio.

Of course, it was not my place to offer advice. Doubtless, in Nashville, a world of opportunities awaited one more songwriter. He'd have been rash to rush up there on a shoestring with a sack of homemade tapes. The Rubes, indeed. But he was thinking about it.

Would he take that plunge? Rather, which plunge would he take? He'd come to a fork in the road, of sorts. The door to his future was now hinged with the added factor of Viola Henley's desires.

I had my garret room again, my upper room above the garage, my little nook, my ivory tower. I had agreed not to smoke in the house, not more than one a day, at any rate, a token promise to which I adhered in spirit, if not to the letter.

The porch steps faced the south and caught the sunshine on the front of the house. Even on a cool day after Christmas, out of the wind, the concrete steps warmed first, while the house itself retained a chill. On such a day, it felt good to sit and bask in the sunlight, to smoke and think and plan for an even brighter tomorrow. As the cypress shade receded and the dew dried on the steps, Floyd moved with his coffee and paper from the table on the screened front porch to the concrete steps outside the door, there to languish and read and observe the natural world around him; a world of mourning doves and mockingbirds, transient cardinals and bluejays, nut-laden squirrels overhead traversing a highway of telephone wires, stray dogs roaming the neighborhood, stalking estrous bitches. I joined him on the steps and we passed the time of day discussing various topics of interest.

On such a day, a fish might fall from the sky, though twice in one lifetime might strain credulity. Walter, on the other hand, was certain to drop by. As I sat smoking on the steps, I heard the spring on his screen door creak open and slam shut. "Here he comes," I said, glancing to my left as Walter meandered in dizzy patterns across the yard toward us with an enormous drink in hand.

"Hey, Walt," said Floyd, "what's happening, bud?"

"Another groovy day," said Walter, weaving in place, "another groovy day by the seashore."

I looked at Floyd. "I feel a song coming on."

"Well, it's another groovy day by the seashore," Floyd began drawling lazy, spontaneous lyrics, "and I'm still on vacation. But I could be having a whole lot more fun. If Katie would come home from bingo."

"Aw, man," said Walt, "you're doing it again. Pete, he's doing it again."

"What, you don't like it?" said Floyd.

Walt took a sip of his drink, shaking his head. "I don't like it."

"If I sang like Tennessee Ernie Ford, you'd like it," said Floyd.

Walter pressed the glass tight against his cheeks as he tipped it back and blew gurgling bubbles into his drink. His red eyes over the rim of the glass watched us, noting our revulsion. "I don't think I have that much imagination," he said.

"One of these days I'm going to learn how to sing better," said Floyd.

"I want to make a movie," Walter announced. "Pete, you can write it up and Floyd, you can hold the camera. I'll direct it and star in it myself."

"I'll bite, Walt," I said, "what's the movie about?"

"All you have to do," he said, "is follow me into my house with the camera. I'll do the rest. No, I'm serious. Listen. A cab pulls up. I get out and walk away. I don't even pay the driver. He calls out to me to pay him the fare and I fall on my face in the yard. He peels off, laying a patch in the grass. I get up and head for the house. The front door looks like it's right there. I keep staggering towards it but it doesn't get any closer."

Floyd chuckled, "Are you staggering or stumbling?"

"I get to the door and try to open it. I lean back to pull myself up the steps and the screen door breaks right off the hinges. I fall again but I get up and go inside. The camera follows me as I pour a big drink, light about five cigarettes and turn the stereo up full blast. Then I start picking up record albums and shaking the records out of the sleeves and they fall to the floor and break. Then I start breaking all my records, throwing them down on the floor and all around the room. Then I go to the kitchen and get a plate of spaghetti. Max is watching me from the corner, he stays out of my way. I take the spaghetti into the living room and I'm eating the spaghetti standing up. Then I hold the plate above my head and watch the spaghetti slide slowly off the plate. Then I dump it upside down in the middle of the floor and the spaghetti oozes down through the pile of broken records. I sit down on the couch and light another cigarette. "Here, Max," I say. "That's the only line in the movie."

"Won't be tough to write the script," I said.

"No, this really happened," said Walt. "I take a sip of my drink and reach for the remote control, turn the TV on real loud. Then I just sit there and stare at the mess I've made of my life. That's the end."

"Return of the Stumbler," said Floyd.

"You think it's not a joke," said Walter, "but I don't want it to be funny."

"Too bad," said Floyd.

"No, I want it to be like a commercial for A.A. or some private hospital that treats alcoholics."

"That's not a bad idea," said Floyd, "a ten minute A.A. training film, called 'Do You Know This Man?'"

"Everything's a joke to you," said Walter. "You never want to be serious."

"We could make that video before I move. All we need is a video camera."

"You're really moving?" said Walt. "Don't move. What about the Rubes? I thought we were putting a band together. I thought you were into it."

"Well, you know," said Floyd. "We'll still get together. We can play at your house."

"It'll never be the same," said Walt.

In a sharper tone, Floyd said, "I can't help it. If you want to do a song today, fine. If not, I don't have time to fool around. I've got to start painting."

"Inside or outside?" Walter inquired.

"Inside."

"Want me to help? I can paint."

"No," said Floyd. "But I'm having a yard sale in a couple of weeks. If you want first crack at the house of bargains, I'll give you the guided tour."

Walter sipped his drink. "Hey, Pete," he said, "he's really moving."

"Yes, Walter," I said. "Indeed he is."

"Where will you go?" Walter stared at me with red, haunted eyes.

"Excuse me?" I said.

He looked away and began blowing bubbles into his drink again. "You think I'm drunk."

"If you don't mind," I said, "I think I'll make a phone call now."

"Go ahead," said Floyd. He moved forward to let the screen door open and I slid past him into the house.

Christmas was yesterday. I had not seen my boys, nor were they home on Christmas Day when I called. I only wanted to wish them happy holidays.

"Are you selling your records?" I heard Walter ask.

"Not if you're going to break them," said Floyd.

I was not familiar with the term, "call waiting." As often as I used the phone, it never occurred to me to keep abreast of the latest development in telephone technology. The intermittent beeping signal interrupting my calls to my knowledge served no purpose. The nuisance did not stop even though I ignored it.

I had reached Arthur on the phone and, in the midst of his very hip recap of the previous day's events, which, to be sure, defied condensation, the infernal buzzing began. I shook the phone, hoping to hear a rattle of some sort, or the sound of gears falling into place, perhaps. In frustration, I juggled the receiver from hand to hand, shifting it to my other ear. In the process, I pressed a button that put Arthur on hold and connected me with Frances.

"Is that you, Pete?" Imagine my surprise to recognize her voice.

"Frances, how did you get on this line?"

"Pete? I didn't hear you pick up. Don't you say hello?"

"I was talking to Arthur, Frances. How is it that I'm now talking to you?"

"Well, you had a holly, jolly Christmas, didn't you? Is he on hold? I'll let you go, then. I just wanted to invite you over for dinner, if you'd like to come. I'm cooking today, and you know what that means."

"Of course, Frances," I said. "But, excuse me, what do you mean 'Is he on hold?'"

"You've got call waiting, don't you?"

"What is that?" I had to ask.

"Where have you been, Pete," she sighed. "What is call waiting? Oh, that's funny. Does your phone have a hang up button? Push that button and say goodbye, Pete and when you let go you'll be talking to Arthur. That's if he's still waiting on you."

"Ok, Frances," I said. I pushed the button and got a dial tone. I called Arthur again but he had stepped out. I left a message on his recorder explaining the accidental disconnection, attributing the bulk of the blame to "Call Waiting."

I had no money to pay for long-distance calls, though I desperately needed to speak to Jack about the clock, in case I didn't make up there, as planned, for New Year's. There was a chance that Arthur might grab a ride with a friend who was leaving for New Haven that same night. Alone, he was not prepared to navigate the city, and the friend would have to drop him off somewhere. Jack couldn't meet him. He was eighty-five and no longer drove his own car anywhere.

Arthur sounded less than keen on going, anyway. Money was tight. Unless he went, I would have to call Jack and tell him neither of us was coming.

The phone was already in my hand. Punching the number from memory, I let it ring and ring, imagining the echo sounding through the vacant halls. Jack seldom answered before the tenth ring. After twelve rings, I set the receiver down. A car pulled up in front. Viola. I decided to wait and confirm Arthur's plans before calling Jack again.

Out front in the sunshine, Viola smiled as she emerged from her car with a covered dish in hand. "Meals on wheels," she sang.

Floyd sprang forward to relieve her of the burden.

"Bean casserole," she said. "My mother made it. You should

have come with me yesterday," she said, "everybody asked about you."

"Welcome back," said Floyd.

She looked at Walt and me, standing by. "I'm not interrupting some kind of male bonding ritual, am I?" she asked, with a coquettish, wrist fluttering gesture.

"We're just sitting out here because it's warmer than it is in the house," said Floyd.

"Why don't you turn the heat on?" she asked.

"What for?" said Floyd. "It's warm out here."

"Not that warm," said Viola.

"Here, sit here," said Floyd, giving up his spot against the door, "feel how warm it is."

"Feel's cold to me," said Viola.

"Oh, Christ," said Floyd.

"I can't help it," said Viola, "I'm cold blooded."

"You want a blanket?"

"No, she said. "Maybe I should go. That way you boys can continue your male bondage."

"Come on, Vi," said Floyd, "be serious."

"Why not? You have time for your friends. Why should I stay here and freeze to death?" she pouted.

"All right," said Floyd. "I'll cut the heat on, even though it's warm as toast out here, even though we don't need it on."

"Don't bother yourself on my account," she said, shivering. "I'll just go home if I get too cold."

Floyd laid an arm across her shoulder. "It's really not cold," he insisted.

"Fine," she said. "Warm as toast."

"There you go," said Floyd.

"You guys are funny," said Walter. "You ought to get married."

"What a great idea!" said Floyd, too broadly sarcastic.

Viola looked away from him, hurt. "I have to go," she said.

"You just got here," said Floyd.

"I have things to do," she said.

"You coming back later?"

"Why? Do you not want me to?"

"I just asked," he said.

Her lower lip quivered with unimaginable sorrow. She kissed him as if she were embarking on a journey.

"See you later, then?" he said.

"Ok." She backed out of the yard, wiping her eyes.

"Yeah, I want to marry her," said Floyd, as he sat back down on the steps.

"Believe me, Floyd," said Walter, "I know what I'm talking about. You two were made for each other."

"Shut up and go get your guitar," said Floyd.

"Don't tell me to shut up," said Walter.

"Well, fuck you, then," said Floyd. "Get the fuck out of my yard and quit bothering me."

Walter drained his glass. "Am I bothering you?" he said. "How am I bothering you?"

"Fucking liquorhead," said Floyd. "Don't move. Oh, no, I'd rather stay here and entertain you on my days off."

Walter retreated, glaring. "You're not well, Floyd," he said. "You're not a well person."

"Yeah, see ya," said Floyd.

He sighed as Walter went back to his own house. "Why did I do that?" he asked.

I lit a cigarette and looked away.

"My nerves are shot," he said. "I fly off the handle at the least provocation." He leaned back in the warm sunlight, closing his eyes. "I'm going to miss this place," he said.

On the last night I spent at my old residence, Jenny had already moved out, taking Bradley with her. Arthur was staying with friends. I sat alone that afternoon in the empty apartment where we'd lived for seven years and worked on the script that I hoped would save my family. What was to become of us now, I wondered. I had given little thought to where I would go, but the rent was three months in arrears and I had finagled my last extension.

That was a New Year's Eve to remember. Arthur and I had decided to go out with a bang. He brought by a couple of friends and a guitar. Bradley made an appearance and left us his boom box tape recorder. As per usual, he had a hot date. On impulse, I walked to the corner phone to call Floyd and invite him over if he was free that evening. His only question was should he bring his wooden xylophone?

That night I was blessed. A footnote to the aftermath of the failure of my marriage was the creation of a song called the Sturdivant Street Blues. Floyd had a copy in his archives of the recording. He played it now and again, for laughs or inspiration. It was a rare take captured; Arthur on the wooden xylophone, me ad-libbing lyrics. If my memory of that night ever dimmed, the tape was there to remind me of the laughter with which we were able to greet that New Year.

Bit late in life by the music bug, that recording, for better or worse, convinced Floyd that he could, indeed, play the harmonica. From that night on, he began to record all his practice sessions. In lieu of music lessons, he had amassed a cassette library of singularly rough and spontaneous recordings. By the time he met Walter, several years later, a backlog of lyrics were taking up space in a drawer, and he had yet to master the harmonica.

"Remember that New Year's Eve?" I said, knowing he knew which one I meant.

He nodded. "How could I forget?"

"You've come a long way since then, kid. You've got your own band now and everything."

"Yeah, it's like riding a meteor," he said.

"Just don't forget the little people," I said, "when you move into Graceland."

Walter's door slammed shut again. He strode across the yard with a fresh drink in one hand and his black guitar in the other. "Let's do a song," he said.

"What song?" asked Floyd.

"Deadbeat Hotel," said Walt, strumming the chords.

"Ok." We went inside and Floyd quickly set up the equipment, placing microphones and setting the dials on the recorder. From practice, he knew that when Walter was ready, that was the time to record. "Let's cut this biscuit," he said.

I kept time on the typewriter case with my brushes. Walter improvised an elaborate intro. Floyd decided to attempt a crooning simulation of Rudy Vallee.

I got a room at the Deadbeat Hotel
I got a girl named Little Nell
She was married to the Farmer in the Dell
Now we got a room at the Deadbeat Hotel

Meet the Rubes.

The days and nights rolled by as in a dream. I had my own concerns. Meanwhile, Floyd was painting, cleaning, organizing the mess in the garage, getting ready for the yard sale. Viola was there a good part of the time. We got along well, the three of us, as long as I made myself scarce. At night, I would slip in through the side door and go up to my room. In the night's dead silence their voices carried through the house; Viola asking him if I was there or not, and Floyd, attuned to the sound of my footsteps, having to guess. "How should I know?" I heard him answer once. "He slips in and out of here like a vampire."

Late at night in my little room I would lie awake and sift through the detritus of my eroded options. New Year's Eve had come and gone. Jack was unsurprised when I told him neither of us was coming. I'd written another long letter to Rico. All seemed quiet on that western front. After weeks of stalling, Jenny informed me that Arthur was seeing a psychiatrist about his depression. Her insurance was good for that sort of thing. The dancing girl was still in the picture, still torturing him with her needs. Bradley was in training to be a fireman. I hadn't heard from Voris. Frances was doing well. Her gunshot wounds healing nicely, she wore her new scars with pride, eagerly lifting her voluminous skirts to display her fish white belly, pockmarked with bulletholes.

Where would I go when Floyd moved? The question ranked with the other great unanswerable questions. My days there were numbered, yet I refused to give in to the feeling of despondency that gnawed like a termite at my vitals. Something always came up. I was determined to roll with the punches, come what may.

The yard sale took place on two consecutive weekends. Floyd, the wheeler dealer, plastered one cent price stickers on items worth less than two cents. Old gallons of paint went two for one. Things he could not have given away, he sold for a penny to passersby.

The early crowd found him ready, despite the threatening weather. When it sprinkled, I helped him haul perishables inside. When it cleared, the two of us carried everything back out.

In the afternoon, when he felt like taking a nap, I kept an eye on the store. The buying frenzy had subsided. Still, a big set of speakers marked at fifteen apiece I let go for twenty. When he woke up I laid the twenty on him. "Thanks," he said, adding the bill to a folded wad, chuckling as he turned all the faces the same way. I thought he might lay a couple on me for helping, but no, he stuffed the bulging wad back into his shirt pocket and laughed as I stood waiting like a bellman in a swank hotel.

"Will there be anything else?" I asked.

That did it. He peeled a fin off the wad and handed it to me, sighing like a parent at the end of his rope.

I was standing in the doorway to his room. He was at his dresser, just inside the door. On top of the dresser was an open mouth glass vase with a thin brown coating of pennies on the bottom. Floyd was tossing his pennies into it. "Pete," he said, "I've been tossing pennies into this jar for six years and there's still only thirty-nine cents in there."

I made an effort to look suitably perplexed.

"Not that I care so much about the pennies," he went on, "though that does irk me. What really gets me is you getting into my silver." He indicated the smaller mahogany goblet where he deposited his more substantive change. "Do I have to hide my change from you, Pete?" he asked.

My token protestations drew a harsh reply. "You think I care if you don't have cigarettes? You think I care you don't have your half a pint? It costs every penny I make just to live. And you, my friend, need cigarettes. You need a half a pint." He tore another five of the roll. "I didn't think you'd do me like that, Pete," he said.

I took the bill from his lingering grip. "The pennies," I said, beginning to explain.

"The pennies are just pennies," he said, turning his back. "It's the principle."

Next door at Walter's, I took his order for a pint of Jim Beam. He threw in a couple of bucks for the trip and I set out for the liquor store, tracing a well trod trail of shame and humiliation.

Which was all right. Which was fine. It was not the first time I ever debased myself. Floyd was a fine one to invoke principles. All well and good to covet a piano. All well and good to assume my complicity.

Relations grew more strained between us as the last days approached. With pressure mounting to get all the work done on time, the pace of the painting and cleaning accelerated. Floyd's landlord, Mr. Demjanjuk, began coming over to check on things, taking a proprietary interest in the old house. Two weeks were left in the month and the place was still full of boxes and beds and furniture, the front yard littered with unsold buckets of paint, rusted car parts, assorted useless objects with the ink on the last clinging price stickers faded to faint smudges. The great pile by the street for the trashmen grew larger and became two piles.

Mr. Demjanjuk seemed like a reasonable man. He and Floyd circled like combatants around the meaty issue of the three hundred dollar security deposit. Floyd intended to quell any resistance on the part of Mr. Demjanjuk to the idea of returning the entire deposit. Amiably, if possible, he hoped, as their relations had been, for the most part, over the years, except for the matter of the van Floyd drove, which he had purchased several years earlier from Mr. Demjanjuk. A minor grudge was still attached to that transaction.

As a sideline, Mr. Demjanjuk bought and sold used work vans,

THE ROUTE

fixing them up in his garage and workshop. When Floyd dropped by with the rent, he used to look at the vans and they would talk prices.

The van he decided to buy was priced at two thousand. The deal Floyd made with Mr. Demjanjuk was to paint the outside of the house for six hundred off the price of the van. He painted the house and when he went to buy the van, Mr. Demjanjuk told him he had already sold that other van, the two thousand dollar van. The white van looked like the same one to Floyd, but Mr. Demjanjuk said it was a different van, a better van, a twenty-six hundred dollar van.

White vans all look alike. He couldn't call his landlord a liar. And it did turn out to be a good van. He bore Mr. Demjanjuk no lasting ill will, but his notions of fairness and justice were bound to the literal terms of his lease, which specified only return of the property in a "comparable condition," a loosely definable term, at best, as a quid pro quo for the return of the security deposit.

He was painting the porch when it began to sink in to me how soon Floyd was going to be leaving. The front porch had always been cluttered and dusty. In the space of a day, it was cleared, cleaned and painted.

I had moved my typewriter out to the porch table. Floyd worked around me as I typed out a letter to Jack. He took great pains to explain to me about Mr. Demjanjuk.

"He's going to try to stiff me. I know it," he said. "Any lame excuse will do. It won't be you, though, will it, Pete? You know what I mean? Don't let it be you. Ok, pal?"

Him calling me pal was a warning shot. The return of his deposit had nothing to do with me. That he was so free with his intimations stuck in my craw a little bit.

Mr. Demjanjuk, I reasoned, might want an experienced house sitter on hand to keep an eye on the place between tenants. I wondered if he had it rented yet, and if so, how soon the new tenants were scheduled to move in?

The hard facts of life contend every man is for himself. If Mr. Demjanjuk could be persuaded to let me stay there a couple more days, what kind of counter offer was Floyd likely to make? Was he concerned in the least with my predicament? Did I but think so, I might have worked a little harder on my invisible man routine.

As it was, I stayed away as much as I could, searching out other avenues of resource and possible shelter. In the winter it was harder, and harder every year to face the prospect of no prospects. My old reliables, Frances, Mr. Willets, Mr. Youngblood; all were happy to see me and welcomed an hour or two of my company, but even Frances, my last best hope, drew the line of hospitality short of taking me in.

All roads led back to Mr. Demjanjuk. In the flurry of activities, my comings and goings attracted no attention. I had tested the waters at Walter's to no avail. He made it crystal clear that I was welcome to visit anytime, but not to stay. Still, the little bungalow was sitting there vacant, waiting for me.

There was an old green rug in Floyd's kitchen, covering the worn gray linoleum. When I came in, he was rolling it up. "Pete," he said, "you want to give me a hand with this? Help me get it out to the street."

I gripped one end and helped him drag it toward the door. An Astroturf facsimile, a durable indoor-outdoor product, the carpet's sudden absence made the kitchen look bare.

"You know," said Floyd, "I found this rug on the side of the road six years ago. Almost brand new, nothing wrong with it, I brought it home, cut it to fit." We tugged the rolled up hulk through the doorway and down the porch steps. Floyd made a vaguely liturgical sign of benediction over the battered green rug. "From the curb thou didst cometh," he said, "and to the curb returneth thou shall."

"Amen," I added, solemn. We dragged the rug the rest of the way out to the street, where the two piles of trash were becoming small mountains.

The rug was somehow weighted with non-lingering symbolism. The sense of vacancy its absence left in the kitchen was accentuated by the dingy gray linoleum tiles, which Floyd attempted in vain to scrub clean with detergent and bleach.

When Walter came by, he was slinging a wet mop across the floors, in no mood for an interruption. Walter, his depth perception impaired, misjudged the distance to the coffee table and spilled his drink trying to set it down.

"That's it," said Floyd, throwing a dirty towel on the spill, "you're out of here." He grabbed Walt by the shirt collar and thrust him through the doorway onto the porch and into the screen door, which flew open as Walt tumbled forward down the steps. Floyd kept a grip on his collar as he went down, restraining himself from inflicting serious harm.

"Go home, Walt," he said, as Walter staggered to his feet, "just go home."

Walter stared out at him from the unfocused depths of his distilled dimension. "I didn't do nothing wrong," he said.

Floyd went back in the house, jerking a thumb over his shoulder at Walter, a signal to me to keep him occupied and out of the way while he worked. I obliged, as I always did when he required my assistance. I sat on the steps, my back to the closed porch door and talked to Walt awhile, thwarting with patient ease his half-hearted efforts to re-enter the house.

When Viola drove up, the two of us fell silent. Perhaps we unnerved her. Perhaps, as she approached us on the porch, we were neither of us in much of a mood for pleasantries. Our responses to her cheery greetings were cordial, if noncommittal. At any rate, her face fell as I nodded that yes, Floyd was inside. A pensive expression followed in the wake of her former smile.

Walt gave me a cigarette as I stood to let her pass into the house. Their voices carried, the tense words echoing through the nearly empty house. "Your friends hate me," she said, "for taking you away from them, from all this. They do. Pete looked at me like it was my fault he doesn't have a place to live. Well, it's not my fault his sons won't have him."

"C'mon, Walt," I said, rising from the steps, "let's go over to your house."

"A drink," Walter said, echoing my very thought.

We granted the lovers the privacy they deserved without a qualm. As ever, I wished them both the best and desired only happiness for them. Of course, I expected his relationship with her to take precedence over our mere friendship, yet I was certain our mere friendship would last, a certainty that Viola seemed to covet, to some degree.

Walt poured me a small drink of bourbon and coke. "Floyd's getting weird," he said.

"The stress of moving."

"Hey, I moved plenty of times," he said, "I never got weird."

The timing was wrong to bring up the bungalow. I sipped my drink and watched him thinking. I could almost read his mind, to the point of predicting his next words. "You can't stay here, Pete," he said. "I already talked to Katie about it. There's no way."

Sometimes the best pitch is no pitch.

"You know I like you, Pete. You're a good friend, but I'm not Floyd. And this ain't the Deadbeat Hotel."

The ice in my glass clinked. "How about another little drink?"

"You drink my booze," he said, "smoke my cigarettes. Now you want to live with me, too, and eat my groceries."

"Walter," I said, standing up, "forget about it."

"Don't leave, Pete." I counted to three and mouthed his next three words as he spoke them. "Katie's at bingo."

Back at Floyd's, Mr. And Mrs. Demjanjuk had stopped by to check on the progress. Mrs. Demjanjuk was appalled by the condition of the bathtub, which badly needed resurfacing. Who was going to pay to have that work done? She wondered.

"That might cost you about a hundred dollars," said Floyd. He and Mr. Demjanjuk were in the kitchen, talking. The oven, Mr. Demjanjuk observed, was also due for a cleaning.

"You just want to whittle down the security deposit," said Floyd. He was cleaning the insides of the kitchen cabinets with a spray bottle of cleaner. "What about the painting? I could have left this place like it was."

"I would have tracked you down," said Mr. Demjanjuk.

"This looks like normal wear and tear to me," said Floyd, indicating the house in general with a gesture.

"When you moved in this house was beauty-ful!"

"Don't argue with him, Bill," said Mrs. Demjanjuk, her voice trailing out from inside the bathroom. Bill. I filed that one away.

"What's it going to take?" said Floyd, chin to chin with his landlord.

"Ok," said Bill. "How about your friend, the writer, what's his name?"

"Pete? He'll move along," said Floyd.

"He offered to do some painting if I let him stay here till it's rented. I don't want him here."

Floyd shrugged. "We're in accord, then, you and me. I clean the oven, these cabinets, what else? I have my stuff out tomorrow and you write me a check?"

Bill nodded. "We'll settle up tomorrow."

I was on the porch, sitting at the table in front of my typewriter when the Demjanjuks came outside. "Hello," I said, standing as Mrs. Demjanjuk threw me a wave on her way out. "Say, Bill," I said, having decided on a direct approach, "I've got something coming up that will dovetail nicely with the painting we discussed. I'm looking at no more than a couple of days. You don't expect your new tenants for at least a couple of days, do you?"

"I don't want you to do any painting here."

"Won't cost you a cent," I said. "One night, then. One more night after tonight and that's it."

Mrs. Demjanjuk tooted the horn on her Mercedes. "I have to go," said Mr. Demjanjuk. "You'll have to find someplace else, mister."

"Foster," I said, "Peter Foster."

"You can't stay here," he said.

"Ok," I said, turning my palms up. I waved to them as they left. Floyd and Viola joined me on the porch.

"I'm fixing to jerk that table out from under you, Pete," said Floyd.

"That's all right," I said, moving my typewriter aside onto an overturned cardboard box. He carried the table outside and loaded it onto the top of the van.

"I can't believe what that woman said to me," said Viola. "When we were in the bathroom she mentioned how repulsive it is, which it is," she emphasized pointedly to Floyd, "she said 'I hope you know what you're getting into, dearie.' She called me 'dearie.'"

"She still whining about the tub?" said Floyd.

"Of course," said Viola, "and men in general. Confirmed bachelors in particular."

"He said we'd settle up tomorrow, whatever that means," said Floyd. "Now I need oven cleaner."

Viola offered to make the run. "What else do we need from the store?" she asked.

"Wine," said Floyd. "Tonight we dance."

"Like old times," I said.

"Pete, after tonight, the party's really over. I'm out of here," he said. "I just want my deposit back."

"That has nothing to do with me," I said.

"After I get the money you can torment Mr. Demjanjuk all you want," he said.

"I can be out of here in five minutes."

"That red suitcase has to go too, and all your toiletry articles out of the bathroom. You've got more stuff in the house now than I do."

"I'll get it out."

"You got some place to go?" he asked.

"Maybe," I said.

"Which means you don't yet," he said.

"Not to worry," I said. I gathered a few items to carry and set out walking in the opposite direction of Frances' place, struggling to put into my step the air of a man with options. As soon as I turned the corner out of sight, I headed up the back block toward Frances'. I thought about her picket fence, standing half-painted through the winter, waiting on spring. She would have other chores that needed doing.

After a couple of drinks with Frances, I helped her hose down Delbert. His incontinence was becoming increasingly troublesome for her, and his favorite chair reeked of formaldehyde, urine and excreta. I wrestled it outside, through two doorways and down the back steps to the yard, where she hosed off the naugahyde with a high pressure hose fixture. Delbert stood naked on the concrete under the hose blast, oblivious to the chill until Frances wrapped a big towel around him. Then he started shivering.

"I wish he'd quit shitting," said Frances. "He's worse than a monkey."

I had a hard time visualizing myself involved with their daily lives again. In my frame of mind, I wanted only to be far away. Yet I faced it squarely. If I could be of service to her, I was working. Work was work.

"I'd let that chair dry out in the sun tomorrow, Frances," I said. "I'll drop by and give you a hand with it, take it back inside for you when it's dry."

"I appreciate that, Pete. Here." She handed me a dollar. "Here's a dollar for your trouble."

"Thank you, Frances," I said, "but do you think you might lay a couple extra on me, say three or four?"

"Well, if you're coming back," she said, counting her purse change. She handed over three bucks in change. "I can't get that chair in by myself," she said. "And it'll rot out there if you don't bring it back in."

"I'll be back," I said.

"Thanks, Pete," she said, "I don't know what I'd do without you, sometimes."

That evening the late sounds of revelry emanated for the last time from the Deadbeat Hotel. Walking home from Frances' I heard Lyle Stone's hoarse gravelly rasp in full argumentative throttle against Floyd, while a guitar gently weeped.

"The Stones," Lyle insisted.

"The Beatles," said Floyd.

"Wrong," said Walter, uninvolved in the rote recitation of their old debate. "Here's Pete," he said, as I approached the door. "Pete, come on in, man."

"Calling all Rubes," said Lyle. He shook my hand heartily. "Here's our drummer. Floyd, give up that drum, boy, let Pete have it."

"Is this the right address?" I said. "My agent said drummers get scale at this gig."

"Mr. Jingles," said Floyd, hearing the change in my pocket. He passed me the drum, a native instrument bound with deerhide, looping the leather neck thong over my head.

"I didn't see this at the yard sale," I said, testing the not so taut skin surface with my fingertips, remembering my halcyon days as Ricky Ricardo's third alternate conga player at the CopaCabana.

Lyle had a couple of beers in him, nothing to set off any alarms, by his standard. He was tapping on the wooden xylophone, trying to figure out a way to play a harmonica at the same time without taking the cigarette out of his mouth.

The room was full of smoke. Walter had at least one cigarette going. I looked at Floyd inquiringly.

"Yes, you can smoke," he said, "but this is the last time."

"Don't listen to his holier than thou shit, Pete," said Lyle, throwing me his pack of cigarettes.

Walter strummed a half-remembered fragment. "Go outside on the porch and smoke like a furnace," he sang, "go outside on the porch and smoke like a train."

Lyle drowned him out with a threatening rendition of 'Dim Lights, Thick Smoke, and Loud, Loud Music,' altering everything but the name of that tune.

"How about 'Massa's in de cold cold ground?'" Floyd suggested. Lyle stopped singing.

"How about this one," said Walt. He strummed some familiar chords and Lyle joined in for a duet of 'Long-haired Country Boy.'

"We going to play 'Stairway to Heaven' next, or what?" said Floyd, as Walter began an interminable segue.

"I'm trying to quit," said Walt.

"Let's not just wander around through the memory of time. Let's get serious," said Floyd.

THE ROUTE

"There's nothing serious about us," said Lyle.

"Do your song, then," said Floyd. "Do 'P-Farm'".

"You mean 'Fourteen Days,'" said Lyle. "I changed the title."

I noted only then that Viola was present, asleep on a large hassock in the corner of the room.

"Yes, her babyness is sleeping," said Floyd. "She doesn't feel well."

"Maybe you should take her home," said Lyle. "We'll wait for you."

"She'll be all right," said Floyd, "if she can sleep through this. Let's do 'P-Farm.'"

"'Fourteen Days,'" Lyle corrected.

"Whatever," said Floyd. He adjusted a microphone, double-checked the recording unit. "The tape is running."

"How does it go? I forget," said Walt.

We weren't going anywhere, it seemed, and then, without preamble, we dropped into a Rubish groove. A transcendent three part mournful harmony arose to bolster and steady my approximation of the rhythm of road gang workers slinging grass scythes in the noonday sun. Lyle's mumbling background undercurrent suggested a distant murmur rolling in over the fields, the wide far fields of peas and greens, where spiritual gospel chants were reduced to doggerel by men of low estate:

Fourteen days I've been on the farm
Picking green beans with my skinny arms
Cut off all my hair and scrubbed me with ice
Said it's to get rid of those pesky little lice
Down on the P-Farm, where I am
Down on the P-Farm, no strawberry jam

On the second take, Lyle managed to get through the last verse without laughing. The tape was running. Floyd dropped back and harmonized, his tensions visibly fading. To capture yet another magic moment on tape for the archives, that was raison d'etre for the Rubes.

"What'll we do when Floyd's gone?" Lyle lamented. "Where will we go?"

Walter looked at Lyle as at some strange crazed beast. He didn't quite know what to make of Lyle even yet and made no reply.

The session wound down. Viola stirred, shifting on her hassock.

"You getting antsy, sweetness?" said Floyd.

"Little bit," she said, sleepily.

"Say goodnight to our friends," said Floyd.

When the beer was gone, Lyle said goodnight. I asked him to give my best to Jane. I had not seen her for awhile, nor them together, for that matter. As I recalled, her house stood in general need of repair. I made a mental note to take a closer look at the house the next time I detoured through her neighborhood.

Walter went home contented, having played well. Floyd unplugged the stereo system last, wrapped cords and wires in neat bundles and carried each piece of equipment out and loaded it into the van. In the end, there was nothing left of theirs inside but the hassock, on which I intended to sleep that night, since the mattress on the floor of my room had been dragged that day to the curb. There was also the jumbo bottle of tabasco sauce, which Viola had discreetly neglected to pack.

They were leaving. Floyd, though vexed that I was staying at least one more night was not about to get into that again, after such a lift with the music. He wanted to say something, but there was nothing else to say.

"Goodnight, kids," I said.

Viola waved, "Goodnight, Pete."

In the dark house I contemplated the manifest errors of my ways. I lay awake with the knowledge of having been consigned by my bosom family to the hinterlands of reality, or, rather, if I could stop dithering, of having consigned myself there, since it was I who had made a profession, even a philosophy, of sorts, of keeping external realities at bay. If I had, indeed, become an embarrassment to my sons, I still had yet to breathe a word to them against my dear ex-wife. Mired in irony, my lips were sealed, while she, unhindered, pursued her campaign to unman me in my boys' minds. To expect my boys to retain the will to remember their dad as they pleased seemed to me like such a small thing to ask.

In the morning, before the Demjanjuks returned, I hid my bags in the attic, which accessed from my upper room. When they drove up, I was outside, tidying up the yard. Floyd had left an assortment of junk in the garage and in the yard. The trashmen were knocking down the piles a little at a time.

I wandered over to Walter's and sat on his porch, watching the scene a little later as Floyd pulled up in the van with Viola. He got out to talk with Bill, who met him in the yard with his checkbook. Without shaking his hand, he wrote the check out on the hood of his car.

He scrawled a signature on the check and handed it over, saying with grudging finality, "I give you this check because my wife says not to argue. I've got a heart condition. And you're the kind of person that likes to argue. You're hot-tempered."

"Hot tempered?" said Floyd.

"You call yourself a painter," Mr. Demjanjuk sneered, "using a wet mop on wood floors. They're ruined now. I'll have to put in carpet."

Floyd looked at the check, nodded, and climbed back into the van. As he pulled out of the drive for the last time, we acknowledged each other with barely perceptible salutes. Bill walked back to the house in disgust. He cast a curious eye over at me and I gave him a nice, friendly wave.

Chapter Twenty-Three
Vagrant or Vagabond

Four days later, Mr. Demjanjuk found my bags in the attic. I had painted the trim on the screen porch doors and the yardwork I had also done was not inconsiderable.

The new tenants, a woman and her teenaged son, arrived as I was emerging from my upper room. I nudged the saloon doors at the foot of the stair open with my red suitcase and typewriter in hand. Disconcerted, Mr. Demjanjuk introduced me as the painter. The woman frowned, her enmity, however unfounded, was instantaneous. "I've been doing some painting," I said, anticipating the question she asked as I answered it, "What's he doing here?"

Mr. Demjanjuk filled the void that followed by holding the screen door open for me. "That's right, he was just leaving, weren't you, Pete?"

I carried my stuff next door to Walter's. He and Katie were both at work. I put my bags on the bungalow side of the house and sat for awhile on their front porch steps. The temperature was a little too cool there in the shade, so I dragged a decrepit lawn chair around to the western side of the house, leaned it back against the warm pink asbestos tiles and sat there in the sunshine for at least an hour before the first patrolcar pulled up.

Two young officers approached, fresh-faced and officious, each with a hand on hip to steady the inelegant bounce of nightstick against leg as they walked across the dry grass and surveyed the crime scene.

"What seems to be the problem, officers?" I asked.

The elder of the two looked younger than Bradley. He glanced once at his partner, then at the house next door. "There's been a complaint," he said.

"A complaint?" I repeated, wondering which cherubic youngster would adopt a bad cop posture.

They conferred for a moment, mumbling. "Something about a peeping tom," said the first officer. The other stood behind him, gazing at the sky.

"Come on," I said, "a peeping tom?"

"We're only doing our job," he said.

"Of course," I said. "I don't blame you fellows. As you can see, I've been sitting, enjoying the sunshine, reading in this chair here." I indicated the well-thumbed paperback dictionary beside the chair. "I'm in violation of no law sitting here reading, am I? As for peeping in windows, I can assure you officers, I haven't the slightest inclination to take up voyeurism at this late date."

"You live here?" asked the second officer.

I consulted my wrist, though no watch was there. "I'm waiting for Mr. Wellington," I said. "He should be home from work any time now."

"Maybe you should move along, then," said the bad cop, the sky gazer, "come back later when he's home."

"No law against reading," said the first officer. "We can't make him leave on just her say-so."

"If it'll make things easier for you boys," I said, making a show of raising my creaky bones up from the chair, "I'll move around to the front, how's that? The last thing I want to do is upset anyone."

"We appreciate that, sir," said the good cop. "We're only doing our job, you understand."

"Not an easy job, is it, son?"

He flashed a boyish grin. I left the lawn chair leaning against the wall and walked around to the front porch. As the officers were returning to their car, its fender marked with the inspirational motto, *"working together, committed to the citizens,"* a second patrolcar pulled up.

"We didn't call for backup," the good cop informed the newcomers. He reached inside for the radio, rolling his eyes for my amusement over the roof of the car.

Several minutes of intermittent static determined in code the four officers' next missions. Another call came in and both cars sped off to investigate.

Walt came home and we had a drink. "Hey, Pete," he said, "you're not trying to move in here, are you?"

"A couple of days," I said. "Come on, Walt."

"Absolutely not," said Walter.

I smoked and waited. For what, I could not have said, the tide to turn, an inspiration, my ship to come in, Godot. At the heart of every art is patience, no less the art of persuasion. I had to hang in there, wait him out. The key with Walter was his loneliness. There was always a key.

"Seen Floyd?" I asked.

He shook his head. "Have you?" He plugged in a cassette tape and stared at the soundless TV screen, flicked through cable channels with the remote.

"I just wondered."

"He'll never come over here," said Walt. "Even when he lived next door, he never came over." He looked around at the walls of his living room, the yellowish paint browned to a dingy nicotine sheen. Chesterfield Brown, we used to call it. Large cracks crisscrossed the ceiling. Peeling paint hung in handkerchief-sized sheets where plaster had bubbled. "This place is a dump," he said.

There was my cue. "We could paint it."

"Who's we?" said Walter.

"I'll paint it for nothing," I said. "There's an offer you can't refuse."

In the time it took him to digest the terms the deal was made. In lieu of five bucks a day rent for two weeks, I would paint the living and dining rooms. He'd buy the paint.

Katie was thrilled at the idea of painting the rooms, although she did not fully appreciate my meticulous preparations. Repairs of the cracked plaster ceiling with spackle and caulk and sandpaper were very labor intensive. "When will you be done?" she kept sighing daily, reminding me of a scene in 'The Agony and the Ecstasy', where Chuck Heston as Michelangelo is painting the Sistine Chapel and Rex Harrison as the Pope keeps walking under the scaffold, complaining, "When will you make an end?"

I slept on the porch, on a cot, the first few nights, since the bungalow room was still off limits, by the landlady's decree. I didn't argue, but it only made sense to make use of the vacant room. After all, it had its own bathroom. Not to mention a desk and a lamp, and a landlady in Arizona.

By the end of the week I was in there. I set up my typewriter on the worn wood desk and stared at it for a long time. With twenty tapes going at once in my head, to tune in one, I had to tune out all others. I scrolled in a fresh sheet of paper and typed Dear Rico at the top of the page, lit a cigarette and tried to marshal my thoughts.

Rico, my friend, the circumstances under which I am writing this letter would defy your imagination.

My letters to Rico invariably employed the same opening line. Same close, as well: As Ever, Pete. At least the middles were different, hopefully neither maudlin nor despondent. Rico knew me. He knew I missed my boys.

Arthur, by my calculations, had attended by now some forty A.A. meetings, at his mother's insistence, or, more properly, forty Adult Children Of Alcoholics meetings. One of the two. I found it exceedingly difficult to picture him submitting to their tepid brainwashing procedures or embracing the cultish fervor of their shared commiserations. Jenny, a ten-year member, was doing her best to plant in his mind the fiction that sniveling at the feet of the deity, Abstinence, was the one avenue left open to him on earth.

Bradley's resentment of me was at least in keeping with his callous facade. Since he was old enough to walk to the bus stop alone, he had required little from me and expected less. Arthur, in my stead, had become his brother's guardian angel, providing him over the years with shelter, money for dates, food, assuming, in short, many of the privileges and responsibilities of fatherhood, covering for me, so to speak, while I struggled in vain to secure a future for them with my script.

"Don't you have a dream to follow, Dad?" When Bradley said that to me, it cut like a razor through the shell of my reserve.

Had the Disney thing panned out, or any one of a dozen potentially lucrative deals materialized, instead of an endless roundelay of hopeful maybes, the script alone might have changed his tune, if he could have only seen my labors produce some results. Too late for that now, Bradley's mind was closed on the subject of Dad.

Jenny, I never blamed for anything until I realized the bitterness with which she begrudged me the respect of my sons.

Did I know her heart was a thorn when I married her? There were signs, but I saw them not. Even when her parents came to stay, did I ever refuse or mistreat her?

Jasper and Hilary, what a pair of New York sophisticates! Alzheimer's time for both of them. Jasper went first, mercifully getting on with it.

I can still see him sitting in his beach chair under an umbrella I had set up for him, a little Panama hat with a green brim on his bald head, pretending to read the New York Times. I left him that way and walked down to the water's edge. A minute later I turned around and he was urinating in the sand beside his chair. I didn't miss him much.

That left Hilary, mother of all harridans. To this day, Jenny insists on holding me responsible for her death, a patent absurdity with no basis in fact. Why on earth would I have tolerated her spiteful acrimony for three years, watching her wither in mind and body into a malevolent creature we had to keep locked away in the living room for fear of her escaping the house and running amok through the streets in a psychotic trance, which she did, once, when she escaped, if doing her in were my intent?

The police found Hilary in a phone booth, shivering in her soiled housecoat, swearing she'd been kidnapped. They brought her back and then had the gall to lecture me on the consequences of negligent care of the elderly.

I could have punched that officer right in the nose back then. I often wished I had. As if I had nothing better to do than wetnurse an incontinent gorgon. Let Jenny explain why I could not work for three years, or whose job it was to wash Hilary's wretched behind, enduring curses that would have turned a lesser man to stone. Ask her who cleaned the walls after Hilary flung turds and smeared coprophiliac handprints in abstract designs as high as she could reach.

Never mind the patience of Job. Had I loathed the woman a thousand times more than I did, I would not have harmed a hair on her head. Many times, had I the inclination, I could have pinched her nostrils shut with two fingers and never wakened her. Each day and night I lived with the opportunity and the temptation.

Even Arthur, at seventeen, wrestled with that temptation. Here was a boy who never brought a friend home all through high school because his crazy grandmother was locked in the living room.

The fabric of our family was unraveling by then. Peter was gone. Arthur did all he could and more to keep the family from breaking apart. "Don't feel alone, Dad, I've thought about doing it, myself," he admitted to me, the day he came home from school to find Hilary's corpse propped up on the couch, her face frozen in a horrified mask of fear, as if the last sight her eyes encountered were the gates of hell opening for her.

I met Arthur at the door that day and pointed to the living room. "By the way," I said, "I didn't do it."

I knew he believed me. With no note of discord between us, we took a roll of Scot towels and a bottle of PineSol into the room and made it presentable, knowing full well the embarrassment the state of Hilary's room would have caused us all, particularly, Jenny, if it were seen by public officials in its full, unmodified glory. It took us a good two hours to remove the encrustation from the walls and furniture. Stains were left, stains no cleaner could ever remove and only multiple coats of paint would cover. I called the police, then I tried to call Jenny, but she was out and never got the message, never knew until she walked in the door as the police and the coroner were leaving.

She looked at me with tear filled eyes, mistrust behind the tears. "You did it, didn't you?" she said.

A bigger man than I might have managed after ten years or so to forget she said that. It was all I could do at the time to let it pass. I only mention the incident now to shore up the defense of my good name against her spurious charges.

I picked away at Walter's ceiling while my mind churned over such memories. What Katie failed to realize about the ceilings was that the plaster texture was peeling off with the paint. The entire ceiling was a flawed surface. Thus far, I had contained the peeling in two quadrants, thinking the rest of the ceiling intact, a mistake I discovered when the separated texture began dropping at the slightest touch in the other quadrants as well. Each chip of the scraper loosened another chip. It went on and on, despite my caulking, despite my stopgap measures to restrict the cancered spectrum.

Was I demoralized? As the days wore on, the ceilings continued to stymy my patchwork, the separation spreading in ever widening gyres like a migratory tumor, malignant to the core, bent on a conflict to the death with me. Demoralized? No, invigorated, braced by the challenge of craftsmanship. For craft will out. Craft is a caulking gun and a texture roller.

Walt said, "Pete, just paint it." We were well into the second week. I had walls and windows still left to paint. If I had a dollar every time he or Katie said they didn't care how it looked, they just wanted it painted, I could have paid my room rent months in advance.

The ceilings were a marvel of ingenuity. They were both very happy with the way I had simulated a texture match in the patched areas. Walter picked a golden tobacco color for the ceilings and walls and a dark mustard brown for the trim. I never saw a couple more anxious to see a room painted. I had the ceilings and a sample area on part of one wall painted when Katie noticed me starting to wash up at the sink.

"Why don't you paint the rest of it?" she asked.

For one thing, the light was fading.

"We'll turn on a lamp," she said.

I told her I was calling it a day. I'd finish the walls tomorrow.

"Tomorrow?" she said, deflated, yet, in her meek way, adamant. "Why can't you finish now?"

To my knowledge, Katie did not have much of a temper. So I stood by in mild shock when she grabbed up the roller from the tray and furiously started rolling an erratic splotch of mustard colored paint on the wall. When the roller was dry, she threw it down in frustration.

"Tell Wall I'm going to bingo," she said, a moment later, in a calmer tone of voice, her old self once again.

From that point on, I felt unappreciated. Walt claimed that he was, himself, a very fine painter and that, had he the time, he would have done the whole job himself. "Hey, it might not look like your paint job," he said, "but at least it'd be done."

The living room windows remained to be painted. "Watching you paint is driving me crazy," said Walt. He was off that Saturday. At four o'clock in the morning, he poured his first drink of the day. By ten, he was showing signs of truculence. "If you were getting paid by the hour," he said, "this paint job would cost me about a million bucks."

"Walter," I said, "it's not costing you anything."

"Too bad I have to go to a party today," he said, "or I'd finish it myself."

A party. What a break for me not to have him underfoot on his day off. His boss, out of some misguided sense of adventure had invited Walt to the company picnic.

Some cronies from work picked him up around twelve in a

pickup and brought him to the party. An hour later a patrolcar brought him home. Walt rolled out of the car, staggering in place by the passenger side as the officer, from behind the wheel, offered him a few words of advice. I set my brush down and watched through the front window, the officer tapping his ticket book against the wheel, ever more emphatically, Walter, safe in his own yard, practicing free speech. "You big asshole," said Walt. "Get out of the car."

He couldn't leave it alone. The officer, plainly weighing his options, revved his idling engine as I stepped outside. Walter shook his fist at the cop through the passenger window, which went up in his face electronically.

"I'll give you one more chance to get out of that car," said Walter, pretending to kick dirt on the tires.

The patrolcar eased forward. "C'mon, Walt," I said, nodding my gratitude to the officer, who departed without a backward glance.

"Who in the fuck are you?" Walter asked, roaring at me.

"It's me, Pete," I said. "I'm painting, remember?"

I helped him inside. "Pete," he said, "where's the paint? I'll help you."

After I wrenched the brush out of his hand, he went to change out of his party clothes, his new shirt and jeans splattered now with brown paint from his struggle with me. He came out of the bedroom wearing a faded green pair of gymshorts and a shirt advertising a theme park called "WALLY WORLD."

Two adolescent teenage girls, a daughter of the City Councilman who lived two doors down from the Deadbeat Hotel and one of her friends, walked by the house while he was changing. I did not think about them as they passed. Their daily treks to the park or wherever they went and back were frequent reminders that life is short and sweet, but of no concern to me, otherwise, except that it registered in the back of my mind, when Walter walked outside, that they were liable to soon come walking back the other way, within a matter of minutes. Then, I looked out the window again at Walter, standing on the edge of his yard, green shorts around his knees, urinating on the public thoroughfare in the very spot where the patrolcar had parked to let him out.

Walt, I thought, if those girls walk by now, it's pokey time.

I went out again, approaching him with caution. A few doors down, a screen door slammed. The girls came out jostling each other and chortling with teenage mirth, no doubt having made an innocent phone call to some shy young boy. "Pull up your pants!" I commanded Walter.

His reflexes responded to the edge in my voice. He did not notice the girls approaching again from down the block and, docile and chastened of mien, allowed me to lead him back to the house. The girls walked past the house again as I closed the front door on their fading giggles.

The timing on that one was so close I had to wonder why it mattered so much to me what happened to Walter. I thought I was doing him a favor, trying to keep him out of jail. Whatever faux pas he had committed at the party that warranted him being removed I neither asked nor cared to speculate. Obnoxious behavior of some sort, without question. A friend of Arthur's who was also at the party, related the anecdote later that Walter, when introduced to his boss' mother, had put a hand on her breast.

That having happened, he was safe at home, reverting to routine, building and hoisting yet another power drink when Katie arrived home from work. I had one window left to paint.

"It looks great, Pete," said Katie, "are you finished?"

"Almost."

"Wall," she said, "I'm going to bingo." She changed her clothes and left.

By the time I finished painting the last window, Walt had passed out in the tub. He wasn't even on the couch. I cleaned my brush in the sink and put my tools in my room. Then I garnered some change, and set out to buy a pack of whatever new brand of generic cigarettes was on sale that week, maybe a buy-one-get-one-free kind of deal. I tore the filters off anyway, long since having forsaken my regular brand.

By the pay phones of the liquor store I stood thinking of Arthur and how long it had been since I'd talked with him. The quarter for the call was in my hand. From where I stood, I could see Eugene's bush around by the back corner of the bowling alley. A strange impulse sent me walking across the street toward it.

Often I had passed by it, ignoring the same impulse, curiosity more than anything else, morbid fascination with the proximity of death. Drawn to it now I approached the bush, determined not to shrink away. Once inside, with my back against the bowling alley wall, I felt the cold comfort of Eugene's basic shelter. Invisible to the world at large, in Eugene's bush, I remembered Eugene, who collected cans.

Little memories that applied to nothing but a small life lived inside a bush rolled over me, like handing empty cans to Eugene one by one out the window of a car Lyle Stone was driving. On a Sunday morning we were taking a ride and rolled up to Eugene's spot by his dumpster. He was crushing cans with a wooden mallet on a stump, filling his garbage bags and his cart. The smile on his face when I slipped him a cold one, shined in my mind like a lamp.

"God bless you boys," he said. Lyle donated weekly to Eugene, all the cans from his floorboard.

From inside his bush, in the confines of his humble world, I remembered the way people looked at Eugene, with indifference or pity or as if he were invisible. To most of the world, he was invisible. God forbid that he might have ever had sons or that they had seen, or, worse yet, never seen him pushing around his heavy cartload of cans.

My exit from the bush was overdue, having slaked a passing fancy and indulged a curiosity, but in maneuvering through the crawlspace, my foot uncovered the corner of a buried piece of cloth. Unearthed, the cloth was a knotted white sock containing a small fortune in nickels, dimes and quarters, amounting to twelve dollars, and a single scrap of lined paper on which was scrawled in a childish hand one work in capital letters, "WILL."

I stayed a moment longer, contemplating my find. All I needed was the spectre of Eugene hanging over my latter years. I counted out three eighty-five for a half pint and got out of there, deciding to toast Eugene's memory properly. Then I heard sirens.

Walking back to Walter's along the road by the park, I had a presentiment of disaster. The firetruck parked in front of Walter's confirmed it.

The fire was out. Wisps of ash floated on the evening breeze. Bradley, on duty that day, stood nonchalantly by the truck with a clipboard in his hand.

"Hi, Dad," he said, with a savage grin as I approached. "This where you were staying?"

"What happened?"

He adopted a professional tone. "Couch caught fire. Smoke damage, mostly. Nobody hurt. Good thing you weren't in there."

The outside wall where the bungalow adjoined was blackened and smoldering.

"Asbestos shingles," said Bradley. "Whole house is contaminated. They'll have to move."

"My script's in the bungalow," I said.

"Oh, we didn't let that burn," he laughed.

"I just finished painting the living room."

He couldn't stop grinning, "Where will you go now?"

"Don't trouble yourself," I said, waving a wrist, "I'll find something."

Walter came striding up then. I introduced Bradley as my son. He nodded to Walt and returned to the paperwork on his clipboard.

"Pete," said Walt, "my house caught on fire, as you can see."

All my paintwork, up in smoke.

"I think it started in the bungalow," he said.

"Walter," I said, "according to the fireman here, the evidence indicates that it started on the couch, where it caught the curtains and spread out the windows to the outside of the bungalow. Nothing inside the bungalow burned, as I understand it."

He went on without hearing me. "You ruined me, Pete," he said. "I'm ruined."

"Walter," I said, "I wasn't even here."

THE ROUTE

"I want you to go away, Pete," he said. "I want you out of what's left of my house right now and I want you as far away from me and Katie as you can go. Go far, far away. Don't even talk to me. Get your stuff. We'll have to move now, but wherever we go, I don't want you coming over for a long, long time."

Walter walked off to join Katie, where she was having an earnest conversation with the realtor, who did not look pleased. I turned to the firetruck, where Bradley had been sitting a moment before with his clipboard, watching the scene with Walter and me, but he was no longer there. I stood in the yard, uncertain what to do or where to go. Next door, at Floyd's old house, a clothesline was strung across the front porch, with a load of washing hanging. My lip curled with involuntary distaste at the sight.

Chapter Twenty-Four
or Knock on Any Door

My feet led me of their own accord up the street to Frances' house, each step a reminder how my route had shrunk.

"The wedding bells ring," Frances announced. "Mr. Delbert finally popped the question."

"How lovely for you," I said. "Will you be a June bride?"

"Are you kidding?" she snickered most maidenly. "We're going downtown before he forgets he asked me."

Voris had called there looking for me and left a number. Frances gave me a sly pinch me and asked, "So who's Mrs. Ferguson?"

I called Voris from Frances' to learn that she had returned from Sanford with Henry. They'd evicted the tenants, a couple of college boys. Henry, having foreseen the eventuality of his return, had videotaped the rooms prior to rental. Unaccustomed to such tactics, the boys, although they had damaged nothing, did not contest the eviction notice and moved out after less than a month.

Voris had work for me, something, at least. Frances, in high spirits, hummed "*The Wedding Song*" while she made me a roast beef sandwich to go.

My things were still in the bungalow. Gambling that Walt would not toss them out in the street, I avoided walking past his house and took a detour down the next street over to Voris'.

She still wore her ball cap skewed to the side.

"Welcome back," she smiled. "Got a job for you, Pete. I can't get his Nibs to do anything."

Henry, still sedated, lay sprawled on the living room couch. He lifted a listless arm in greeting.

"Time for his nap," Voris explained. "Talk to me while I water my garden. I've weeds to pull."

"I'd be happy to pull some weeds for you."

She showered her neglected garden with a fine mist from a hose sprinkler. "Henry's crazy," she said. "You knew that, didn't you?"

"Yes, Voris," I said.

She had the flame on her lighter turned up high and it flared like a blowtorch when she lit a cigarette. The smell of burning hair wafted faintly on the breeze.

"I wish they'd shipped him back to that concrete jungle where he came from," she grumbled.

"Voris," I said, "what, did you sign him out?"

"Ah, hell," she muttered, "you're no fun."

The chores she had in mind included painting several rooms as well as some regular yardwork. I laid it out for her in brief, the chores I was willing to perform in return for a roof over my head and three eighty-five an hour, minimum wage at the time, knowing she wouldn't go for it, also knowing that once we started haggling over minimum wage, I was in there.

"How long are we talking?" asked Voris.

"Not long," I assured her.

She found that humorous. "Say that again," she cackled.

"Not long," I repeated, with a straight face.

Henry voiced no objection, mentioning only that the security alarm self-activated at nine p.m. What this bit of data meant to me was a curfew. I was to be in by nine o'clock or locked out for the night. No amount of logic or reason could prevail upon him to disconnect the side door again.

I retrieved my bags from Walter's without incident. He was asleep on the charred remnants of the couch. Katie was packing small things into boxes. She had been crying.

"We have to find another place," she said. "We've been evicted."

"Katie, if there's anything I can do," I said.

She forced a feeble smile. "Too bad about your paint job, Pete. It did look good."

The ceiling, blackened with soot, was cracked and peeling again in a few new places.

"Walt doesn't blame you, Pete," she said. "He knows it's his fault. He was drunk."

"Don't give it a thought."

"You better go before he wakes up, though. He's still mad."

I promised to keep in touch.

A week went by, a week and a half. I pulled weeds, raked leaves, painted a bathroom. The curfew bit was hard to take. Not that I was such a night owl, but even to step outside for a smoke or a breath of fresh air required virtual dismantling of the governing apparatus. For Henry, whose slumbers consumed roughly twenty hours a day, the placidity of his new environs was perfect.

"He doesn't say much anymore," Voris observed.

By nine o'clock, I was in or out. That wore very thin. I slept in the den, on one of the couches, near the sliding glass doors Henry had wired shut.

Walter and Katie moved without revealing to me their new address or their new unlisted number. I felt like an inmate in some weird asylum, with Henry getting up at odd hours, making his vigilant rounds, checking all the electronic signals before returning to bed, and turning off all the lights. Something had to turn up soon. I kept waking up in someone else's limbo, and returning to it every night.

I seldom slept more than an hour or two at a time and I was not allowed to type, the noise being a distraction and a hindrance to lethargy. After lights out, I read by flashlight, a biography of Abe Lincoln from Ray Fletcher's library. Admonished not to waste electricity, or batteries, as it were, I bought my own flashlight batteries and hid them.

A knuckle tapping on the sliding glass door woke me about

two a.m. Mr. Willets was there, holding a note up to the glass: EMERGENCY – CALL FRANCES.

I had given Mr. Willets' number to Frances in the hope that she would never dial Voris' number. Drunk or sober, I could not have her calling there, tying up the phone as she was wont to do, the phone which never rang. My tenure was tenuous enough. Mr. Willets had agreed to take an occasional message, though he never expected to be awakened in the wee hours.

Message received, I thanked him through the glass. His demeanor warned against an encore.

Against all wisdom, I used Voris's phone to call Frances. Delbert had had a stroke. An ambulance had taken him to the hospital. "Please come, Pete," Frances implored me. "I need you here."

The commotion, such as it was, which woke the entire household, consisted of one quiet phone call. As concisely as possible I tried to explain that the call was in response to an urgent summons from a friend.

Puzzled beyond any hope of understanding, Henry asked, "You have to go to court?"

"If you leave now, you may as well pack your bags," said Voris.

"Yeah, pack your bags," said Henry. "People trying to sleep around here."

Ok, I thought, roll with it. I gathered my things, forswearing any parting shots. I tipped my hat to the pair of them, a gray fishing hat that Clarence used to wear, gave the wilted brim a snap, and waited outside for the cab Frances had promised to send.

The house lights went dark again before the cab arrived. I stood in the gloaming, looking across the street at Clarence's old house. Sold months ago, repainted, and occupied now by a different family, it was still Clarence's house to me. Perhaps, I thought, I was not changing fast enough with the times.

The cab took me to Frances'. I carried my bags into her house. She gave me a twenty for the driver and I brought it out to him, demanding some change.

"It's only a five dollar ride, Frances," I said, giving her back a five. "Use some discretion. These cabdrivers are robbing you blind."

"Oh, Pete," she sighed, delirious with grief, "what'll I do? I don't know what to do."

"Hang in there," I said. "You'll get through this."

Delbert's condition stabilized. We spent a grim night in the waiting room, Frances in her double wide wheelchair awash in a blathering sea of tears, while I shepherded her through the maze of forms required for Delbert's hospitalization.

She could not bear to be alone during those first seventy-two hours. I handled everything for her, arranged for groceries and booze to be delivered by taxis at more reasonable rates, stepping into the role of major domo with barely a ripple of uncertainty.

February was almost over and her monthly funds were low. I took that very much into account and employed the thrift of my ancestors in her behalf. The least I expected was a little bit more than being locked out of the house.

When her monthly check arrived she decided to take a cab to Daytona. Out of the blue, Daytona. Two hundred bucks one way in a cab.

"How long do you expect to be away this time?" I asked, nonplussed. Every couple of months she hired a private cab to visit her sister in New Smyrna Beach. This time, Daytona. I didn't think much of it.

"You'll be away for a couple of days, then," I said, when she didn't answer. I was thinking ahead, in terms of Delbert's condition and so on. Slow to grasp what she meant when she said, "I'm locking up the house," I half expected her follow up by giving me a key.

"You do want me to hold the fort here?" I said.

"This fort don't need holding," she said, with a sudden steely eye contact that skipped the rest of the story. "I want to thank you for all you've done for me, Pete."

"But," I prompted her.

She didn't shrink, "But you can't stay here."

"Frances," I said, "I'll get Delbert's room ready."

"It's ready," she said.

Her regular driver, Buzz, came and loaded her into a stationwagon cab. I climbed in with my bags as well and insisted on a ride back to Voris'. She couldn't refuse me that.

"Pete, look in on Mr. Delbert from time to time, won't you?" said Frances. "He's all alone down there in that hospital."

"Sure, Frances, " I said. "I'll give him your best regards."

"Thanks, Pete," she said, without irony. "You're too good to me."

A hard freeze was forecast for that night, but Voris and Henry stood firm and refused to allow even storage space for my bags in their garage.

Mr. Willets let me leave my bags on his back porch for a couple of days. No more, he cautioned, and I took him at his word.

Walter wasn't hard to find. I met him at the liquor store. "Hey, Pete," he said, "how are you? Stop by sometime and see our new place, why don't you?"

"Walter, where you live?"

He told me his new address and invited me to drop over later.

His new neighborhood had none of the pastoral pine grove quality of his old abode, no shade trees gracing the front yard. There was no front yard at all, and only a little side yard for Max.

"Like living in a shoebox," said Walt. I ducked my head as I entered, observing the exceptionally low ceiling. "A couple of months here and we'll find a better place."

"Looks like it could use a paint job," I ventured.

"You didn't say that, Pete," he said. "Don't jinx this place, man. It's bad enough."

I laid my cards on the table with Walt, about Frances, Voris, the whole bit. "Have a heart, Walt," I pleaded.

"Absolutely not," he said, unmoved.

That night I slept in his truck, bent across the bucket seats like a contortionist. Katie rousted me at five a.m. She had to drive the truck to work. My back and lower joints were killing me.

Walt went to work at eleven. In all sobriety, before he left he forbade me to sleep in the truck.

March freezes are wet and windy. Bone chilling cold like an

ague beset me. All day I tried to shake the stiffness out of my lower joints but it felt like it had set in for good and that terrified me. Another night like the last one and I could come down with something serious, chilblains, or pneumonia. My legs were going numb.

To keep warm, I walked to the hospital, lingering there a good part of the day. Delbert was doing better. He asked how I was doing.

"Good enough to walk down here to see you."

"Thanks, Pete," he said.

"You'll tell Frances, when you see her again, that I came to see you?"

"Where is she?" he asked.

"She'll be along," I said. "She sends her best."

Walt worked until seven. In the evening, I watched television with him and Katie until they retired around eleven. Then I repaired to my office, a booth in the all night Krystal down the block.

I could nurse a cup of coffee there all night if need be. With quarters enough for two calls, I dialed Viola's number first, chatted a minute with her and asked to speak with Floyd.

"Hey, Pete," he said, "what's up?"

"What's up? Let's see," I said, shivering, "not the temperature."

"You don't sound so good, Pete. Are you all right?"

"A little nippy out here."

"Out where? Where are you?" he asked, at last.

"At the Krystal. In the phone booth."

"That's where you're staying?"

"Say, kid," I said, "any chance of me spending the night in a warm garage?"

He paused for half a beat, not long enough. "That's not in the picture."

"In your van?"

"No. Look, Pete, are you hungry? I can bring you some stew," he offered.

"Never mind stew," I said, "how about five bucks."

"Pete, I got stew for you, not five bucks."

"Stew, then," I said. "I'd love some stew. You know I appreciate it, kid."

"There's nothing else I can do," he said. "Call Arthur."

"That's another story," I said. "How's everything else, by the way? Viola sounds cheery."

"She's fine."

"Any word from Nashville?"

"I'll bring you the stew, all right Pete? About fifteen minutes."

Of course, I was grateful, despite the harangue that came with the stew. "Call Arthur," he said. "You can't hang out all night at the Krystal, a man your age."

"You can't put me up in the garage for one night?"

He handed me a brown bag with a jar of stew in it. "Not my garage," he said.

The stew warmed my hands through the paper bag. Now, I thought, if only I were hungry. Some time ago, I had ceased to eat, it seemed, and had begun to exist without daily sustenance.

He meant well, Floyd did. He and Viola were at least concerned enough about me to bring me stew. "Call Arthur," he repeated. "Pete, before you call me back, call Arthur."

My reasons for not calling Arthur boiled down to one: I hated to burden him. With my last quarter I called him. He was home and invited me over.

On my next birthday I would have qualified for a senior citizen's bus pass granting unlimited access to all buses at no charge. At that moment, though, I had to tell him, I did not have sixty cents for the bus.

"No problem," said Arthur, after a brief consultation on his end. He prevailed upon a friend to drive him down to pick me up.

"You look a little rough, Dad," he said, as I climbed into the back of a Yugo. "Have you been sleeping in phone booths again?"

"Good to see you, too, son."

"What's in the bag, Mr. Foster?" asked the driver, a corpulent youth named Gabe.

"Stew."

"Ah, stew!" he exclaimed, pressing the accelerator. "Any crackers with that?"

Knowing Viola, I guessed that her package, in all probability, did indeed contain crackers.

"Crackers, too," I nodded, stealing a glance at Arthur to share a secret smile. A nod was as good as a wink.

The two of them devoured the stew and crackers. After Gabe said goodnight, Arthur and I sat up late, talking.

"Well, Dad?" he said.

I turned my palms up in defeat. "It's not my town."

His sigh was far too weary for such a youth. "Won't be the first time we've been evicted," he said, with a hollow smile.

"Arthur," I said, "do you know what a fine chef makes in New York?"

"A godzillion times what I make. Dad, I know what comes next, the clock pitch. I'm not ready for it. I barely make rent here. I can't even think about New York. I've got other problems."

"The girl?"

"What have you heard?"

"Nothing much."

He looked up at the ceiling fan, turning in slow circles. "That about sums it up," he said. "Want a beer?"

He brought a couple of cans out of the kitchen.

"I understand why you never turn to me for advice," I said.

"For predictable advice," he corrected.

"You might have given me a chance, son. My experience with women is somewhat vast."

"The women of today are different, Dad," he said.

"No, son," I said, "they're not."

"I won't argue," he said. He wanted to read a poem to me that he'd written for Peter, part of a series of poems he'd written, one for each of us in our family. He brought a sheet of notebook paper out of his bedroom and stood clearing his throat. He took a sip of beer.

"Brother of mine—" he began. His voice broke and he read no

further. I rose and put my arms around him as he fell against me in tears.

I didn't know what to say. Some time ago, Bradley asked me once where Peter was buried. I offered to take him there some day, but he said that wouldn't be necessary. He just wanted to know where it was.

When Peter died, I grew extremely overprotective of Bradley. Every time I looked at him I saw both him and Peter. Physically, they were so much alike, and their natural affinity toward each other so pronounced. My perception at the time was that Peter's death had affected Bradley more deeply somehow, than it had Arthur.

"All those years," I said, "I failed to recognize what a blow it must have been to you, too."

The poem was a morbid ode to death, beautifully written, in a prescient imagistic mode.

"It's not just Peter," said Arthur, composing himself. "It was everything, you and Mom at odds, shall we say, and me in the middle raising my heartless brother, who, shall we also say, holds you in low esteem. The worst was finding no will in myself to defend you to him. No will at all. Then a woman came along, pregnant, married, aborted, divorced, though not necessarily in that order. You and Mom and Brad, my bosom family, are, oh, so worried that somehow, she'll mess up my life. But it's my life. I can mess it up if I want to."

"Arthur," I said. I yearned to say something uncommon for once, something he could take to his heart but I spared him my gratuitous, predictable speeches and asked him only, "Why you?"

Why you, my son?

His shoulders rose and fell once. "Why not?" he muttered.

"This isn't your town, either, son," I said. "New York. That's where you belong."

"Sure, Dad," he said. "I'll get to packing."

"The clock alone could bring in ten grand."

"Ah, the fabled clock," he said. "For twelve years now I've been hearing about the fabled clock. Is it buried at the bottom of the sea? How is it you've managed not to consummate that quest?"

"Timing is everything."

"Dad," he said, without the faintest trace of a smile, "don't ever run out of mottoes."

I drained my beer and he brought out two more.

"So what's your plan, Dad? You do have some sort of plan?"

"The plan," I said, pausing to think of one. "The plan is to hang in there until something gels with the script. Any day now I should be hearing something from Rico."

"Oh," he said, "that reminds me."

"Did Rico call?"

"No. Brace yourself, Dad. Your script came back."

"Came back?" A silence deep and solemn as the grave stretched between us. I shook it off. "Just when you thought it was safe to go back in the water," I said. "Where is it?"

"Sorry, Dad," he said, retrieving the thick manila envelope from the front room table. "I'm surprised you didn't notice it sitting there."

"I didn't expect it," I said, carefully opening the package and extracting a letter from Rico. "Let's see what he says."

"Dear Pete," I read, "much as I hate to return your screenplay, I can't in good conscience keep it tied up any longer. It's not fair to you, my friend. An agent I'm not. I'm a horn player. Jerry loved it, but you know how these things go. We fell through the cracks, pal. What can I say? I thought we had him. I'll call you in a couple of days at your latest new number. You do get around. All the Best, Rico."

"Well," I said, folding the letter, "that's that."

"You ok, Dad?"

"Sure," I said. "Don't suppose you have anything stronger than a beer around here."

"I thought you might be dropping by," he said. "It so happens some passing stranger left some vodka in the freezer."

I noticed immediately as I thumbed through the script that my most recent revisions had never been inserted into Jerry's copy. No wonder, I thought, they might have made all the difference.

"I'm going to bed, Dad," said Arthur. "Make yourself at home."

I made a drink and wondered where those ten pages were, floating around in infinity somewhere, useless of themselves. Times of greater adversity had found me steadfast in the past. I was with Arthur now, at least for awhile. Things weren't so bad.

I slept very little that night or the next few nights until Rico called. I stayed close to the phone as the days went by. Arthur and I enjoyed each other's company and joked about the script, the clock, and other things. He seemed to have put aside his depression for the nonce. I hoped he would not succumb to ennui, prayed he would find in himself the strength to overcome it.

As his spirits seemed to revitalize, the script's rejection began to fade in my mind, as a prominent issue. Still, when Rico called, the tide of hope came rushing back.

Talking to Rico was like talking to Norman Vincent Peale. "Pete," he said, "I loved your script. Marilyn loved it. We both loved it. It's a gem. What can I say? It's just not happening."

"Maybe I could punch it up some."

"Don't, Pete," he said. You're past it. What's your next project?"

"To tell you the truth," I said, "I've been thinking a lot about my boyhood on Staten Island."

"Not that far back," said Rico. "Gee, Pete, I'm snoring here. What about the fat lady? You don't want to go too far back."

"What are you saying?"

"The stuff in your letters, Pete. That's some neighborhood. Maybe you can make a book."

"I write screenplays, Rico," I said. Under the circumstances, I wasn't quite sure how to respond to a suggestion out of the blue that I might just as well now attempt to tackle my memoirs.

"Pete," he said, "listen to me. How many years before you start collecting Social Security?"

"Four," I answered, "four years."

"What else can you do? I got all your letters saved in a box, Pete. And it looks to me like you got a book here. Marilyn thinks so, too."

"Rico, who'd believe it?"

"Hey, what do you got to lose?"

After he hung up, I thought about his suggestion, counterbalancing his optimism with my current status. I needed to build up my route again. Frances' fence was still waiting to be finished. Her guilt over locking me out would cost her dearly when it resurfaced one fine day. I owed it to myself to square that up. Aside from her, the old neighborhood was about played out.

A new route was in order. I had to get up to Staten Island, somehow. More than ever, the clock felt like my last best hope. Meanwhile, Arthur needed me.

Knock on any door, wasn't that my old motto? That, and tally ho? My memoirs, there was an idea, something to do with my leisure time. Ok, Rico, I thought, what have I got to lose?

ABOUT THE AUTHOR

Kevin Wilson is the founder and chairman of Barnyard Productions, whose first release, The Rubes-Undisputed, proves that almost anyone can make a record. Barnyard Books is a division of Barnyard Productions.

ABOUT GREATUNPUBLISHED.COM

greatunpublished.com is a website that exists to serve writers and readers, and remove some of the commercial barriers between them. When you purchase a greatunpublished.com title, whether you receive it in electronic form or in a paperback volume or as a signed copy of the author's manuscript, you can be assured that the author is receiving a majority of the post-production revenue. Writers who join greatunpublished.com support the site and its marketing efforts with a per-title fee, and a portion of the site's share of profits are channeled into literacy programs.

So by purchasing this title from greatunpublished.com, you are helping to revolutionize the publishing industry for the benefit of writers and readers.
And for this we thank you.